THE BIODOME
GARDEN BOOK
Patricia Watters

Books by Patricia Watters

THE BIODOME GARDEN BOOK
WAIST-LEVEL GARDENING

ARMOUR

ARMOUR PRESS
THE BIODOME GARDEN BOOK
Copyright 2011 by Patricia Watters
First Edition

CONTENTS

ABOUT THE AUTHOR

Patricia Watters is committed to energy conservation and wholesome lifestyles. Log homes and solar greenhouses are complimentary to her philosophy of life. Her objective in creating the BIODOME GARDEN, and passing on the information so that others can benefit from her research, is an effort to help others enjoy a healthful, environmentally-friendly way of life. Ms. Watters became involved in creating an effective passive solar greenhouse system in 1982 while pursuing an interest in growing vegetables year-around that would use a minimum of water. Subsequently, she developed the BIODOME GARDEN, which includes a 900-gallon aquaculture system for heat absorption, radiation, and humidification. Ms. Watters and her husband live in a hand-built log house in the woods of Oregon. Their only source of water is rain water, which is collected off the roof and flows into an 8000-gallon under-ground cistern.

1 WILL YOU BE PREPARED?

Why Build a BIODOME GARDEN?

That's probably the first question you'll ask yourself after studying the dome-covered structure on the cover of this book. Well, for starters, let's consider some sobering facts before returning to that question. It took from the beginning of the human race until 1830 for the global population to reach a total of one billion people. That's not so extraordinary. Lot's of time was involved. However, it took only one-hundred years more—from 1830 to 1930—to add a second billion people. Things are beginning to pick up a bit. Then, in just over thirty years—from 1930 to 1960—you guessed. Another billion people were added to the earth's population. Now comes the sobering part of this little exposition. Only seventeen years later, by 1977, we added a fourth billion. Eleven years later, you guessed it—five billion people on planet earth. 1999 saw another billion, and by 2012, the earth's population is expected to reach seven billion human inhabitants.

That, in a nutshell, is the dimension of the population problem. Now you ask, what has this population problem got to do with building a BIODOME GARDEN? The answer: Food! With the world population growing in giant leaps and bounds, it's highly questionable whether food production can increase fast enough to keep up with population numbers. The prospects definitely appear gloomy. Agricultural economists believe that the world food production has reached a turning point in the race with population, that any further food increases will come at greater and greater costs because we are pushing nearer the limits of potential food output based on present agricultural technology. These economists caution that we should not let the success of the 1960s and 1970s cause overconfidence in the 1980s and beyond.

Now for some statistics. At the farm level in the United States, prices received by farmers have declined in real terms since World War II. This indicates that food farm prices have generally moderated global inflation by rising less than other prices. In the future, however the trend may reverse, and real farm prices could increase annually as population climbs. Over the long haul the main worry is whether food production can increase fast enough to keep up with population numbers. To compound the problem, millions of acres of productive farm land, both in the United States and abroad, have been converted to nonfarm uses, and this combined with soil erosion has had a serious impact on available land for food production. So the answer to the question, "Why build a BIODOME GARDEN?" is—build it for self-sufficiency, to produce your own food. But that's not the only reason. Let's look as some food facts and fallacies.

Food Facts and Fallacies:

Now that we have established that there is a population growth and food problem, we must consider what effects this has on the quality of the food that reaches the grocery. Much of the non-farming expansion in recent years has had a duel negative effect on food production. Not only are our foods grown in soils stripped of natural fertilizers, but those products which do reach the grocery shelves are of questionable value.

With a BIODOME GARDEN, you are not only able to produce food for your own independence and self-sufficiency, but you can produce food of high nutritive value, grown in soils that have not been stripped of their natural minerals. Now, here are some other things to consider while we're on the subject of food value. You, the consumer, are probably not aware that the major drug companies own the vitamin companies, and these drug companies recommend people for the Food and Drugs Administration. This Board of Directors sets up the FDA labeling laws which define the following:

ORGANIC: "Anything that contains a carbon molecule." That is, 100% organically grown whole wheat bread can be grown with DDT pesticide and still be termed 'organic' by the FDA because DDT contains carbon molecules and is therefore *organic* by FDA labeling laws. The products of every food processor are *organic* according to the FDA, because they contain carbon molecules.

NATURAL: "Anything which comes from natural sources," i.e. everything in the universe is natural, including chemicals, pesticides, herbicides etc., because they came from natural sources.

RDA (Recommended Daily Requirement): This is the minimum amount needed to sustain life, not health.

PERCENT OF NUTRIENT: The percent of nutrients listed on the label is rated at the time of harvest, not processing. Most nutrients are essentially destroyed before ever reaching the table.

ASIDE FROM FDA LABELING LAWS, THERE ARE OTHER POINTS TO CONSIDER. YOU MAY NOT BE AWARE THAT:

FRUITS AND VEGETABLES purchased with surfaces that feel greasy may have been in cold storage anywhere from 5 to 7 years. These foods have been gassed in a nitrogenous gas which leaves a waxy residue, but which can preserve foods for up to 15 years.

TIME RELEASED is a term which is widely used and misused. All vitamins are technically *time released* because the body does this automatically as vitamins are absorbed when the body needs them.

ASSOCIATED FOOD FACTORS, of which there are over 50,000 yet undiscovered, are not present in processed vitamins. These food factors, which are present only in fresh food, are essential for sustaining life. When deficient in these factors, health deteriorates.

A VITAMIN A OVERDOSE as termed by the government is equivalent to eating 3 chicken livers. However, chemical vitamins can produce a toxic overdose of vitamin A because they're lacking the Associated Food Factors which are present in fresh food, and which gives the body the natural tendency to reject what it does not need.

ENZYMES, which must be present for any process that takes place in the body, and are present in every cell, are permanently destroyed at 122 degrees F. Water boils at 212 degrees F, so that when foods are boiled, all enzymes are destroyed.

MORE THAN 700 DANGEROUS CHEMICAL ADDITIVES are used to emulsify, synthesize, hydrolyze, stabilize, pasteurize, tenderize, texturize, artificially flavor, and color and condition the food we purchase in the grocery store. What it boils down to is that only through *controlled gardening* can we be assured of maintaining high nutritional potencies in the food we eat. The BIODOME GARDEN provides this means.

What is a BIODOME GARDEN?

The BIODOME GARDEN, when properly constructed, is an organic growing system capable of supplying animal and vegetable protein and nutrients—unlike the typical greenhouse which is basically a seed starter. The BIODOME GARDEN is a design of superior strength, engineered with a high degree of structural integrity, not a flimsy structure highly susceptible to wind beating. Structurally, the dome is the most superior form of construction. The translucent dome over the BIODOME GARDEN admits the sun's shortwave radiation while trapping heat, and at the same time, it resists high winds, and sheds snow, and can, in fact be completely buried in snow several feet deep, without collapsing.

The atmosphere within the BIODOME GARDEN is naturally humidified with a wind-powered ventilation system, which circulates the air within the unit, creating a natural growing environment. The curved shape of the dome allows heat to rise to the peak and be exhausted my means of a wind turbine, which at the same time, creates gentle air currents. In addition, the hotter the air within the dome, the faster the turbine turns, exhausting it quickly, while at the same time drawing in fresh air through the large side vents in the fiberglass dome.

Deviating from the normal greenhouse setup, the BIODOME GARDEN is not a complicated unit requiring extensive electrical ventilation and humidifying systems, which subject the plants to wide swings in temperature—a *hot house* to wilt and bake plants. And unlike the standard vegetable garden, the BIODOME GARDEN does not require tilling, weeding, stooping or extensive watering and care, but is rather a weed-free, waist-level, moisture-retaining, potting soil garden capable of absorbing, storing and radiating heat for a stable growing environment.

Probably the greatest energy savings of the BIODOME GARDEN is the small amount of water needed to maintain a vegetable garden at optimal growth. The system requires approximately seven gallons of water per day during the hot summer months, and less than four gallons during the winter months, depending on regional temperatures and humidity.

With the BIODOME GARDEN, a family can realize substantial savings in food bills by growing fresh organic vegetables (by the true sense of the word), fruit, mushrooms and animal protein, while reducing the amount of canning and freezing through a longer growing season. Along with feeling a great sense of gardening pride and satisfaction, one also has the security and independence of having a permanent near year-around growing system available to provide fresh produce, while combating inflation in food prices.

Once the basic principles are understood, you'll be ready to construct your own BIODOME GARDEN growing system, a system that can stand as an independent unit, or one that can be attached to your existing home for a pass solar walk-in garden that will trap solar energy to help heat the home.

Basic Principles of the BIODOME GARDEN

The BIODOME GARDEN incorporates all of the principles of a biome--a plant and animal community in a dynamic equilibrium. Chapter 2 will delve into it more thoroughly, but to summarize, the circular layout of the raised vegetable beds, with the translucent fiberglass dome above, takes maximum advantage of the sun's warmth. Because solar collectors achieve their maximum potential when tilted at a 90 degree angle to the sun's rays, the dome shape is the most perfect shape to act as this collector because it allows full solar radiation to be received, both daily and seasonally, with the sun's movement across the sky.

Beneath this 16-foot-diameter, by 12-foot high dome, a mini universe teaming with life exists. Aquatic animals, including freshwater mollusks and crustaceans provide a protein food source. These aquatic animals exist on other aquatic animals, insects, larvae and plants which inhabit their world. Vegetables, fruit, mushrooms and herbs provide an organically grown food source rich in natural vitamins and minerals. These vegetables and fruit and aquatic plants give off the oxygen needed by both aquatic and land animals, and insects which dwell within the BIODOME GARDEN.

Beneath the soil of the raised vegetable beds, and within the compost bin, earthworms loosen debris while dropping high-nutrient castings, and their tunneling holes allow water, nutrients and oxygen to filter down to the root zone. While thriving on the nitrogen-rich soil and water provided by the fish tank, the earthworms in turn become a valuable source of fish food.
This mini universe creates its own microclimate. As the sun warms the atmosphere within the BIODOME GARDEN, warm air particles rise with the natural configuration of the dome, converge and descend, causing air currents. Moisture from the 900-gallon fish tank rises, collects on the underside of the dome, and runs back toward the raised vegetable beds, while the water from the fish tank delivers natural, organic nutrients directly to the root zone through the irrigation ring. Watering at the base of the plants results in healthier plant growth by eliminating moisture on the leaves—a common cause of mold, mildew and other greenhouse diseases.

Roots absorb and store this high-nutrient moisture, acting as reservoirs. Through transpiration, leaves give off water vapor which mixes with sunlight, forming misty clouds. These clouds collect on the dome and fall back toward the soil below, completing the cycle. Carbon dioxide given off by the decaying matter in the compost bin is absorbed by the plants through their leaves, utilized, and again given off by the plant roots. This carbon dioxide combines with water in the soil to form a weak acid which acts as a solvent for soil minerals needed for plant growth.

Because water has the highest heat capacity per pound of any ordinary material, the 900 gallon fish tank absorbs and releases the heat equivalent to 40 gallons of oil over a 150 day heating season. Masonry walls, rocks and earth masses, along with the water volume within the BIODOME GARDEN, act as solar heat collectors and storage areas, radiating the absorbed heat into the biosphere during the night. This heat, combined with the heat produced by the compost bin, helps provide winter warmth. The reverse takes place during the warm summer months when the water in the fish tank acts as a heat absorber, helping cool the air within the BIODOME GARDEN. When all elements are combined and working, the unit provides an energy-efficient means of producing food that is free of pesticides and chemical fertilizers. It is a unit capable of producing quality fruits and vegetables, with a minimum of water, on a limited area of space. It is also a place for leisure living and taking time to smell the flowers.

2 PRINCIPLES OF THE BIODOME GARDEN

Components of the BIODOME GARDEN:

Before building your own BIODOME GARDEN or attempting to create a BIODOME GARDEN adaptation to an existing greenhouse system, you must learn the principles of the system as a whole. It's important to understand what part each component of the BIODOME GARDEN plays in relation to the composite BIODOME GARDEN as an ecological unit or mini-universe.

The basic principles of the BIODOME GARDEN were described in the previous chapter. The diagrams below, and the alphabetical referencing which accompanies the diagrams, will describe in greater detail the solar and ecological principles involved in BIODOME GARDENING as well as explain the relation and interaction of the plant and animal kingdoms within the structure. Once the system as a whole is understood, customized adaptations can be incorporated for individual needs.

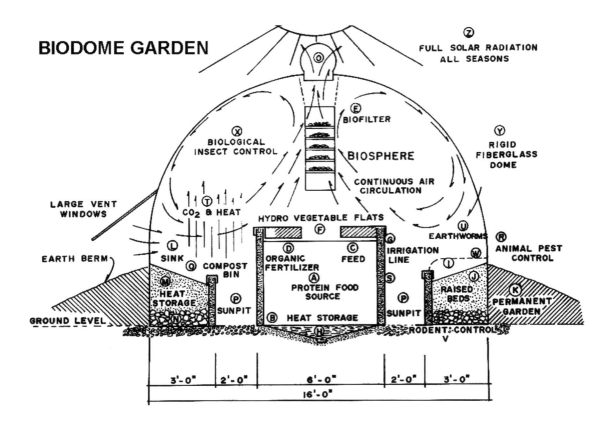

BIODOME GARDEN

(A) **PROTEIN FOOD SOURCE:** Aquatic animals provide a high protein food source and/or a cash crop as ornamental aquaria species. These species include Japanese Koi, which is an edible or ornamental carp, several other varieties of carp, tilapia, catfish, ornamental freshwater lobsters, oscars and gouramis, as well as edible snails.

(B) **900-GALLON FISH TANK:** The 900-gallon fish tank not only serves as a habitat for the aquatic animals, but it acts as a heat storage area as well. The speed with which water can absorb heat, and the large amount of heat it can hold in relation to its volume, make it an excellent heat storage medium. This system also works in reverse during the warm summer months, when the water acts as a cooling medium, when the heat from the air is absorbed into the water which is then cooled during the night. Continuous evaporation of water from the fish tank also acts to cool the unit as well as to humidify the atmosphere within the BIODOME GARDEN.

(C) **AQUATIC ANIMAL FEED:** Plant life, algae, plankton, minnows, insect larvae, tadpoles, earthworms, water insects, vegetable cuttings and garden insect pests make up only a small portion of the available aquatic animal food. Pelleted fish food can also be substituted for natural fish foods.

(D) ORGANIC FERTILIZER: Microscopic plants and animals are introduced by inoculating the tank with a few gallons of natural pond water. The growth of algae, plankton, aquatic plant life, aquatic animals, animal excrement, and minerals in the water combine to form a nutrient-rich, organic fertilizer, high in nitrogen and other minerals needed for plant growth.

(E) BIOFILTER: The specially-designed biofilter inhibits the growth of algae in the water through aeration, while the cedar slats and oyster shells, which the circulating water passes over, help maintain a pH level conducive to aquatic animal growth. The sludge trap at the bottom of the biofilter collects the sediment, which is drained into the compost bin, assisting in the breakdown of plant cuttings into compost.

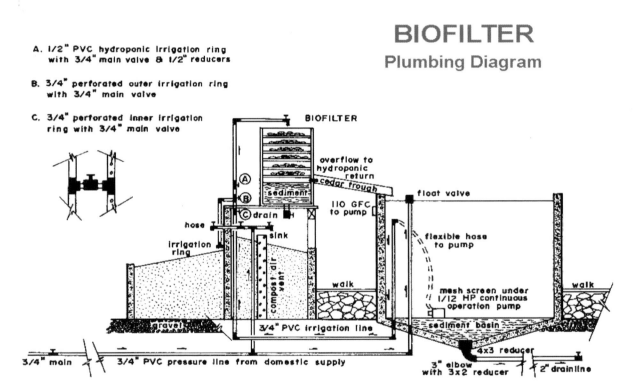

BIOFILTER
Plumbing Diagram

A. 1/2" PVC hydroponic irrigation ring with 3/4" main valve & 1/2" reducers

B. 3/4" perforated outer irrigation ring with 3/4" main valve

C. 3/4" perforated inner irrigation ring with 3/4" main valve

(F) HYDROPONIC VEGETABLE FLATS: Circulating hydroponic troughs are located above the fish tank. In these troughs, plants receive nutrients as water passes through gravel, over the plant roots, and back into the fish tank. Certain varieties of plants adapt and thrive in hydroponic systems. Chapter 7 will discuss a few of the more common plant varieties.

(G) PERFORATED IRRIGATION RING: Nutrient-rich water from the fish tank is pumped through a perforated irrigation line to the plant roots in the vegetable beds by means of a submersible, continuously operating pump.

14

Before entering the perforated line, the water from the fish tank is routed through the biofilter to clear it of excrement and plant debris so that the holes in the irrigation ring don't clog. However, if you intend to incorporate a hot tub system instead of an aquaculture system, you would not include a perforated irrigation ring, but instead a solid line under the soil through which the hot water from the hot tub would be circulated by means of the pump, warming the soil for cold-weather growing.

(H) SLUDGE TRAP: Sludge from decomposing plants and fish excrement build-up in the water, collects and settles in the conical base of the fish tank. This sludge can be easily drained from the bottom of the tank by means of a gravity flow line and a standard two inch gate valve. The sludge can be drained and collected into a bucket or small reservoir and used as a natural fertilizer on the vegetable beds or dumped into the compost bin.

(I) VEGETABLE FOOD SOURCE: The circular configuration of the raised vegetable bed allows for north-east-south-west orientation of sun and shade loving plants. This circular configuration also creates ideal conditions for companion planting by pairing mutually beneficial plants, while also separating plants that attract the same garden pests. The concept of companion planting is discussed in Chapter 8.

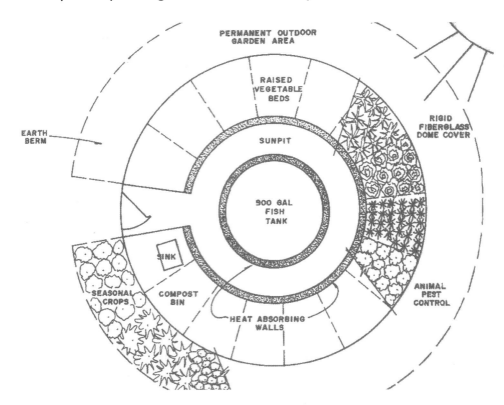

(J) RAISED VEGETABLE BED: The circular raised bed can be prepared to provide *potting soil* gardening. The waist level height of the bed eliminates crouching and stooping, and the vegetable bed is virtually weed free, which also eliminates the need for tilling. Close, intensive planting of crops in the bed (see Chapter 8) produces superior vegetables. Leaves from plants shade the soil, while acting as a living mulch, reducing moisture loss and preventing extreme fluctuations of soil temperature, depending on location.

(K) EARTH BERM PERMANENT GARDEN: An optional second circular bed surrounding the BIODOME GARDEN (not shown on the cover photo) acts as an earth berm for added insulation to the interior raised beds. Permanent plantings such as strawberries, asparagus, and other all-season plants, benefit from evening heat radiating from within the BIODOME GARDEN, extending the growing period from several months to year-around.

(L) UTILITY SINK: The sink in the BIODOME GARDEN enables the gardener to trim and wash plants on the spot, resulting in fresh, clean vegetables brought directly into the kitchen—no dirt and mess in the kitchen sink.

(M) HEAT STORAGE: The concrete inner wall of the vegetable bed, the 900-gallon fish tank, and the BIODOME GARDEN exterior masonry wall, as well as large rocks beneath the vegetable beds, earth, and water masses within the BIODOME GARDEN act as solar heat collectors and heat storage areas. These heat storage masses radiate the absorbed heat into the *biosphere* during the night, thus extending the daily growing period.

(N) LARGE ROCKS: Large rocks placed beneath the vegetable bed creates a heat mass, absorbing heat and storing it until the temperature of the vegetable bed drops below the temperature of the rocks when the heat is released through the earth mass above, warming the vegetable bed.

(O) WIND-POWERED VENTILATION: Good ventilation is important for proper temperature control. To be effective, the venting system should promote the natural flow of air from a low entry to a high exit throughout the greenhouse. In the BIODOME GARDEN, the side openings are placed low, and the wind-powered turbine on top removes excess heat as it rises in a gentle, continuous exhaust. Plants are not subjected to constant blowing by fans, and the system is not dependent on electricity for ventilation.

(P) SUNPIT: The area between the raised vegetable beds inside the BIODOME GARDEN and the fish tank in the center of the structure acts to create a sunpit. The gravel passageway within this area, as well as the concrete walls of the raised vegetable beds and the fish tank, and the water inside the tank, collect and store additional heat for evening release. An optional earth berm surrounding the structure helps hold heat inside.

(Q) COMPOST BIN: The convenient compost bin provides a catch-all for plant trimmings, kitchen scraps, manure, and ashes. Water from the sludge trap at the bottom of the biofilter gives the needed moisture for the process of decomposition. Fungi and bacteria take nitrogen from the air and add it to the soil thus transforming it into materials for plant use in making protein foods. During this process of decomposition, organic materials can reach a temperature of 131 degrees Fahrenheit or higher. This gives off additional heat while forming rich humus for the vegetable beds.

(R) ANIMAL PEST CONTROL: Birds, rabbits, gophers, deer and other wild animals are excluded from the raised vegetable bed of the indoor garden unless brave enough to enter through one of the ventilating windows. Most are not. Digging animals like moles and gophers are prevented from burrowing into the circular vegetable bed by a layer of heavy rock, which is placed at the bottom of the vegetable bed before adding the soil.

(S) SOLAR HEAT COLLECTORS: The dark concrete walls of the raised vegetable bed, the fish tank and the exterior BIODOME GARDEN acts as solar heat collectors, trapping and holding heat for night-time radiation.

(T) CARBON DIOXIDE: Carbon dioxide, released by the decaying matter in the compost bin, aids in plant growth within the BIODOME GARDEN. Through the joint action of sunlight and chlorophyll, carbohydrates are produced as carbon dioxide enters plant leaves through tiny pores and mixes, a process called photosynthesis.

(U) EARTHWORMS: Beneath the soil of the vegetable bed, earthworms loosen debris while dropping high-nutrient castings. Their tunneling holes allow water, nutrients, and oxygen to filter down to the root zone. These earthworms multiply rapidly in the almost perfect environment within the BIODOME GARDEN. While thriving on nitrogen-rich water from the fish tank, the worms' castings create fertilizer for plant growth. These worms in turn can be used to supplement the food diet of the fish in the fish tank.

(V) RODENT CONTROL: Rodents such as moles and gophers cannot tunnel through the base of large rocks and gravel beneath the raised vegetable bed, so they cannot destroy roots or root crops.

(W) MUSHROOM BINS: The warm, dark, damp environment of the area beneath the utility sink is an ideal growing atmosphere for the production of edible mushrooms. Stacked mushroom trays assure a continuous source of vitamin-rich food as well as a delectable gourmet treat. The *mushroom compost*, which remains when the crop reaches maturity and stops producing, is an excellent animal feed, savored by pigs, cattle and chickens and possibly fish food, although that has not been determined.

(X) BIOLOGICAL INSECT CONTROL: Beneficial insects can be introduced to, and maintained within, the BIODOME GARDEN as a non-chemical means of insect control. Predacious insects such as lady bugs, lace wing, and preying mantis feed on the harmful plant-eating insects such as aphids, mealy bugs, spider mites, their eggs, larvae and scales. The placing of frogs and toads, companion planting, smoking, and spraying with hot pepper or other solutions, are other biological means of controlling insects. These and other insect control methods are discussed further in Chapter 8.

(Y) RIGID FIBERGLASS DOME CONSTRUCTION: Glass, being optically clear, allows the sun's direct rays through, while fiberglass scatters the rays into a diffuse pattern, which is preferable for plant growth. The dome also incorporates the superior strength of dome construction with the practicality of rigid fiberglass design. The hemispherical roof admits the sun's shortwave radiation into the biosphere within. These short waves strike surfaces which absorb and emit long waves or heat radiation, and the dome traps the heat. In the hot season, heat rises naturally to the peak of the dome and is carried away by the wind turbine, which spins faster as heat builds. During the cold months the dome offers protection from frost as well as creating a natural airflow or circulation as heated particles rise with the natural configuration of the dome, converge and descend.

(Z) SOLAR RADIATION: All passive solar energy systems collect energy, store it, and transfer it to the point of use. When sunlight strikes the surface of an object, a portion of the light is absorbed and changed into heat energy. Usually, dense materials such as concrete, are better conductors of heat than porous materials such as wood. Air or water can carry heat from warm surfaces to cooler ones through convection heat flow. As the air warms, it rises and expands, giving off heat to surrounding objects. With the BIODOME GARDEN, the fiberglass dome collects the sun's energy and stores it in the mass of the soil in the vegetable bed, the outer and inner concrete walls, the rock and gravel in the sun pit, and the 900-gallon water tank. The circular layout of the vegetable bed with the translucent fiberglass dome above takes maximum advantage of the sun's position year around, as solar radiation is received daily and seasonally.

Of course, there are just some times of the year when the sun can't get through at all, which means there may be temporary interruptions to your growing season. And not every part of the country provides a temperate climate conducive to year-around growth. But with a BIODOME GARDEN the growing season of almost any part of the country can be extended far beyond that of an outside garden. But even when the "sky falls in," growing under the dome is just a matter of waiting for the snow to melt. Your growing dome, nestled securely under whatever depth of snow comes with old Jack Frost, will still be intact. Two feet covers the dome below. Six feet wouldn't have made a difference, except to the little plants struggling for light. But, alas, the sun does come out again, and all is well.

BASICS OF PASSIVE SOLAR BIODOME GARDENING

3

The concept in a nutshell:

Passive solar systems introduce a different set of concerns to the solar consumer than do active solar systems. Passive solar heating generally involves energy collection through south-facing glazed areas. Energy storage is in the building mass or in special storage elements, and energy distribution is by natural means. These systems function with minimal use of pumps or fans. With passive systems, performance depends on correct design and construction and not just component reliability. In designing a passive system there are certain passive solar heating rules of thumb.

According to the Department of Energy, any solar greenhouse must include the following five elements in order to be considered a complete passive solar heating system eligible for tax credits: (1) a collector; (2) an absorber; (3) a storage mass; (4) a distribution system; and (5) a control system. The design of the BIODOME GARDEN incorporates three of these, and the design of the BIODOME GARDEN ROOM (see below) incorporates all of these. Items 1, 2 & 3 should be incorporated into any solar greenhouse system. Items 4 & 5 make the system eligible for tax credits if the unit meets certain Department of Energy criteria.

The 5 Elements of the Passive Solar System Include:

(1) A COLLECTOR: The passive solar greenhouse must be able to collect the sun's radiation, and this solar collector's efficiency is determined by how successfully it converts sunlight into useful heat. This efficiency is not constant. It changes from season to season and from day to day, as the outdoor air temperature and the amount of available sunlight changes. It is important that there be a good southern exposure for optimum collection.

(2) AN ABSORBER: The unit must have the means of absorbing heat and radiating it into storage masses. The absorber of a passive system is usually the darkened surfaces of the walls, floors, and water-filled containers within the greenhouse. In the winter, sunlight passes through the windows (or fiberglass dome of the BIODOME GARDEN) and warms the darkened surfaces of the concrete, brick or rock floor, masonry walls and water-filled drums or reservoirs. Some heat is absorbed into the thick concrete, brick, and water masses, where it will remain stored until the indoor temperature begins to cool after the sun sets. At sunset, the greenhouse will remain warm as long as it can draw on the heat in its storage elements. The storage elements will continue to supply heat until they are the same temperature as the air inside the greenhouse.

(3) A STORAGE MASS: The unit must be able to store the collected heat for later release. When the sun isn't shining, some method of storage of accumulated heat is required. With an adequate storage system, the sun's heat collected during the day may be used at night or on a cloudy day. The three most frequently used materials for solar thermal storage are water, masonry and rocks. Water is not only an inexpensive heat storage medium, but it has the highest heat capacity per pound of any ordinary material, and it is approximately 5 times as effective as masonry. The amount of masonry or rock exposed to sunlight should be 5 times the area of south-facing glazing. The more masonry or rock exposed in the space, the smaller temperature fluctuations from day to night. Rocks should be nonporous and of uniform size. Round rocks provide channels for air circulation so air flow through the rocks is uniform. Masonry should have a minimum thickness of 3 inches to minimize temperature fluctuations. Direct sunlight should be diffused by using a translucent glazing material or a number of small windows that admit sunlight in patches.

(4) A CONTROL SYSTEM: There must be a controlled means of maintaining constants in temperature and humidity levels and of preventing loss of heat during the night. A constant source of airflow through ventilation is important during the hot months to prevent overheating in the greenhouse.

(5) A DISTRIBUTION SYSTEM: There must be a means of distributing the released heat for home use. This can be achieved through fans or natural convection flows from the greenhouse to the house.

Meeting the 5-Element criteria with a BIODOME GARDEN

(1) COLLECTOR: The rigid, translucent, fiberglass dome of the BIODOME GARDEN receives solar heat while giving optimum tilt both seasonally and daily. Because collectors achieve their maximum potential when tilted at a 90 degree angle to the sun's rays, the dome shape, with its curved surface, can hold this angle regardless of the position of the sun, and is therefore ideal for this purpose.

(2) ABSORBER: The dark surface of the raised, circular concrete vegetable bed of the BIODOME GARDEN, the several inches of gravel in the "sunpit" area between the vegetable bed and the fish tank, the soil mass in the vegetable bed, and the volume of water in the fish tank, act as efficient heat absorbers. The darker the surface, the greater the heat absorbing ability, so the dark concrete silo staves are idea for this purpose. For optimal heat absorption, if attractiveness is not an issue, the concrete surfaces of the silo staves can be coated with black asphalt emulsion.

(3) STORAGE MASS: The water in the 900 gallon fish tank of the BIODOME GARDEN is the primary thermal storage area, employing an effective thermal storage medium. This quantity of water will absorb, and then release the heat equivalent of 40 gallons of oil over a 150 day heating season. With a requirement of 1 to 2> gallons of water necessary per square foot of collector, the water volume to collector surface area is more than adequate. Other storage masses within the unit include the earth mass of the raised circular vegetable bed, the masonry walls of the vegetable bed, the masonry wall of the fish tank, the dense rocks beneath the vegetable bed, and the gravel in the sunpit walking area between the fish tank and the raised vegetable bed.

(4) CONTROL SYSTEM: The wind-powered turbine at the top of the fiberglass dome draws in outside air through ventilating windows in the side of the dome and allows excess heat to be removed during warm seasons. The hotter the air is inside the BIODOME GARDEN, the faster the wind turbine turns. This, along with constant evaporation of water from the fish tank, aids in cooling the unit further during the hot season, while the water itself also absorbs some of the excessive heat, thereby helping in the cooling process. Conventional greenhouses require elaborate systems of fans and thermostats and humidifiers to do what this simple dome-wind turbine combination design does naturally.

(5) DISTRIBUTION SYSTEM: This is where the BIODOME GARDEN unit as a single unit falls short where tax credits are concerned, as the unit is not attached to the house and cannot be considered for supplementary home heating. However, the BIODOME GARDEN ROOM, as described below, fills this requirement as it is designed to attach directly to the house, preferably to the kitchen for convenient access to fresh herbs and vegetables at the cook's fingertips. With this design, natural convection flow and/or one small fan (optional) allows heat trapped within the BIODOME GARDEN ROOM to flow into the adjoining house.

Incorporating a BIODOME GARDEN ROOM

Details with photos of how to construct a passive solar greenhouse that is eligible for tax credits, such as the BIODOME GARDEN ROOM, are not included here, but the following diagrams will give you a plan to follow for a retrofit, if you would be attaching it to an existing home, or for a system that could be incorporated into the design of a new passive solar home. But if a hot-tub/ornamental garden is desired instead of a vegetable garden, the BIODOME GARDEN ROOM might be connected to a family room or master bedroom, where it is convenient during the winter months. Whichever way you go, the dome for the BIODOME GARDEN ROOM would have to accommodate the elongated design. One way could be to purchase a half dome, then use long panels of fiberglass to form a Quonset hut design that would attach to the house. The Quonset section is only 16' from the peak of the dome to the house, but a lot of thought would have to go into it, perhaps even the help of a fiberglass manufacturer in the area, who could make a section that would attach to the half dome.

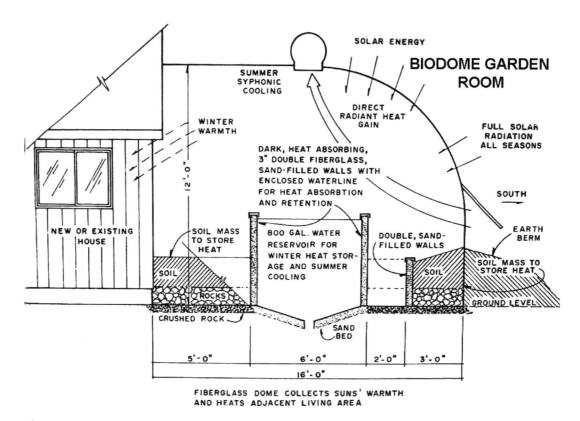

SOLAR ENERGY

BIODOME GARDEN ROOM

SUMMER SYPHONIC COOLING

DIRECT RADIANT HEAT GAIN

WINTER WARMTH

FULL SOLAR RADIATION ALL SEASONS

DARK, HEAT ABSORBING, 3" DOUBLE FIBERGLASS, SAND-FILLED WALLS WITH ENCLOSED WATERLINE FOR HEAT ABSORBTION AND RETENTION

SOUTH

NEW OR EXISTING HOUSE

SOIL MASS TO STORE HEAT

800 GAL. WATER RESERVOIR FOR WINTER HEAT STORAGE AND SUMMER COOLING

DOUBLE, SAND-FILLED WALLS

EARTH BERM

SOIL

SOIL

SOIL MASS TO STORE HEAT

ROCKS

CRUSHED ROCK

SAND BED

GROUND LEVEL

12'-0"

5'-0"   6'-0"   2'-0"   3'-0"

16'-0"

FIBERGLASS DOME COLLECTS SUNS' WARMTH AND HEATS ADJACENT LIVING AREA

A BIODOME GARDEN ROOM can be added as a retrofit or incorporated into a new home

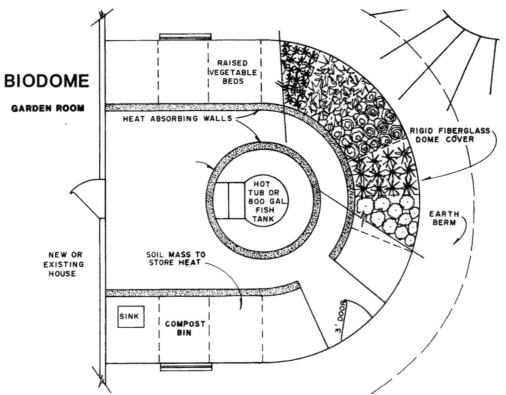

BIODOME

GARDEN ROOM

RAISED VEGETABLE BEDS

HEAT ABSORBING WALLS

RIGID FIBERGLASS DOME COVER

HOT TUB OR 800 GAL FISH TANK

EARTH BERM

NEW OR EXISTING HOUSE

SOIL MASS TO STORE HEAT

SINK

COMPOST BIN

3' DOOR

The layout shows an elongated design that would need a half-dome with a filler panel

24

The photo below illustrates several important elements of the BIODOME GARDEN. These include the fiberglass dome, which receives and collects the solar heat, the dark gray concrete walls of the fish tank in the center, with its 900 gallons of water, the mass of the vegetable bed, which acts as a heat absorber, the "sunpit" access area between the raised bed and the fish tank, which traps and holds heat, and the soil of the raised bed, along with the water in the fish tank, which stores heat for later release.

Plants thrive in the diffused light beneath the dome

STEP-TO-STEP GUIDE TO BUILDING A BIODOME GARDEN

Start With A Solid Foundation

If the area where you plan to build your BIODOME GARDEN is sloping even slightly, you will have to do some excavating to make it level. Scrape out the area to a depth of 12" and push the topsoil into a pile, to be used when filling the vegetable bed. Check the area for level using 2x4s of a length that reaches across the area, and a long bubble level. Or if you have access to a laser level, that would be helpful. You want your completed BIODOME GARDEN unit to sit square.

Trenching for the water and drain lines

(1) Prepare the ground: The BIODOME GARDEN will be constructed on a bed of 3/4" gravel. But before adding the rock, you will need to dig out trenches to a depth of 12" or more for the water and drain lines. There should be an incoming waterline from your source of water, which will split into three lines: one line will go through the bottom of the fish tank and end with a float valve that cuts off the water when it's at the level of the valve; one line will go to the utility sink, and one line will go to a hose bib under the utility sink. You could also add a forth line to a hose bib outside the BIODOME GARDEN for watering the earth-berm vegetable bed. The outgoing waterline from the bottom of the fish tank will split with one line going to the perforated irrigation ring along the perimeter of the raised vegetable bed, and one going to the biofilter (see page 38 for photos of the Biofilter). There will also be a 4" ABS drain in the center of the conical concrete bottom of the fish tank, which will connect to a 4"-3" ABS reducer, which will then connect to a 3" drain line that will terminate in a large valve for draining the sludge from the conical bottom of the tank.

27

(2) Complete the water and drain lines: All plumbing must he set in place before the concrete bottom of the fish tank is poured so that the PVC pipes and the drain outlet in the center of the tank will be sealed with concrete. The end of the center drain line will be fitted with a large faucet that can be opened for drainage (see photo below). With a conical base as shown on the diagram of the Biofilter on page 37, the drain line only needs to be open for a matter of seconds in order to drain out the sludge that will collect in the conical base of the fish tank. However, be sure to place a round section of screening over the drain to prevent fish and other aquatic animals from being sucked out when the drain valve is opened. Inside the tank, a float valve, connected to the end of the incoming PVC waterline at the desired water-level height, will allow fresh water to replace the water that leaves the tank with the sludge (which is very little water), and through the perforated irrigation line in the circular vegetable bed, and through evaporation and humidification. The float valve should be set well down from the rim of the tank because if the water's too high, the fish will jump out. The outgoing waterline is connected to a pump, which pumps the water from the fish tank into the perforated irrigation line and into the Biofilter, which then drains into the troughs of the hydroponic vegetable bed that will span the top of the tank as shown in the photo on page 39.

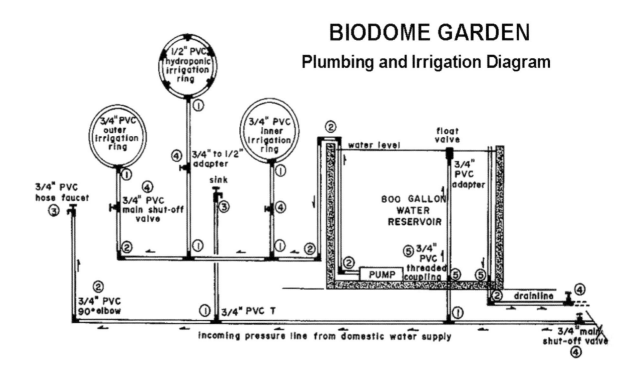

Faucet for draining sludge from the tank

(2) Level the Ground: After excavating to make the ground level, trench to at least one foot for the PVC waterlines and the ABS drain line, and connect and glue all sections of the lines that go below grade. After the lines are backfilled, spread 3/4" crushed rock (the size gravel you'd use for a driveway) to a depth of around 4" and level it the same way you leveled the ground, by using long 2x4's to spread the gravel, and a laser level to check it. Then tamp it down to compact it for a good, solid base. This can be done by using the edge of a long 2x4, or renting a tamper from a local rental store. To prevent dirt and gravel from getting into the water and drain lines while working, cap them temporarily, without gluing them, or in the case of the drain line, stuff a wadded cloth into the opening.

Excavation and leveling is complete, and a bed of gravel is laid out

(3) Stub out the water and drain lines: The black, 4" ABS drain pipe in the center of the gravel circle in the photos above and below will ultimately be cut flush with the bottom of the fish tank. However, while preparing the gravel base, allow at least 12" of both the ABS and the PVC pipes to stand upright until the exact bottom of the concrete, conical-shaped fish tank is determined. The two stubbed-out PVC lines that are near the ABS drain line in the photos will come up through the concrete bottom of the fish tank--one as an incoming waterline from your water source, and the other as the outgoing waterline from a small water pump in the bottom of the fish tank. This outgoing line will split with one line going to the circular, perforated irrigation lines in the raised vegetable bed, and one to the Biofilter and the hydroponic troughs, where the water will return to the fish tank. Of the two PVC lines in the lower right of the photos above and below, one line will go to a utility sink inside the BIODOME GARDEN, and the other to a hose bib under the sink.

Black ABS center-drain and white PVC incoming and outgoing water lines

30

A second hose bib can split off from the waterline that goes to the utility sink and terminate in a hose bib that can be placed on the outside of the BIODOME GARDEN for convenience, especially if an outside raised garden planting bed is constructed, which would encircle the BIODOME GARDEN. Although an outside planting bed is not included in the BIODOME GARDEN on the cover of this book, it is highly recommended that you add one to your own BIODOME GARDEN as it extends the planting area significantly, while allowing for tall plants, such as corn and vegetables like peas and beans that grow on trellises. This outer raised vegetable bed can be constructed of landscaping stones, which would be an attractive addition to set off the BIODOME GARDEN.

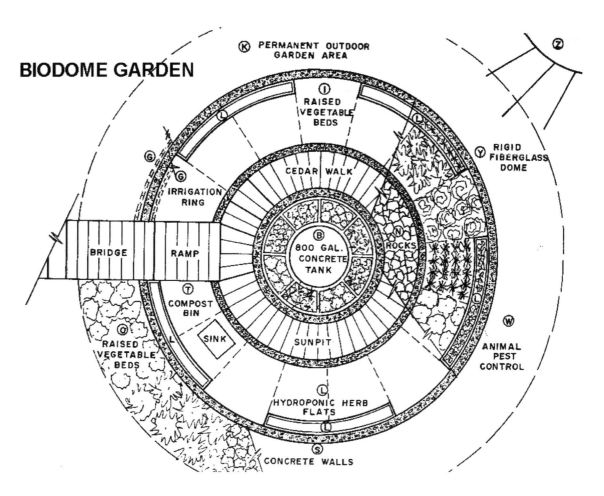

Layout of the concrete walls of the raised vegetable bed and the fish tank

(5) Prepare the fish tank: Before stacking concrete retaining-wall blocks, or setting silo staves in place (your choice, for the vegetable beds), the fish tank (or hot tub) must be constructed or brought in and set in place. A tank with a conical concrete bottom makes it easy to drain the buildup of sludge that collects in the bottom of the fish tank. This conical base should be prepared by concrete specialists who know how to form a conical shape, which will be 6' in diameter, 4" thick, and with about a 6" drop that slopes to a 4" ABS drain with a 4" to 3" reducer and a 90 degree elbow (see the diagram of the Biofilter in Chapter 2). The fish tank inside the BIODOME GARDEN on the cover of the book, as well as the walls of the vegetable garden, are constructed using concrete silo staves, which can be purchased from several vendors around the country (see links in the Appendix), and offered for sale (or even for free just to haul them away from the site of old and abandoned silos), in farm and ranch publications, and on Craigslist.

Setting the concrete silo staves into a ring for the perimeter of fish tank

(6) Set the walls of the planting bed: Silo staves are perfect for constructing the 30" high walls of the vegetable beds. One course of staves will complete these rings and allow for the soil in the raised beds to be 24" deep. The use of staves create a strong structure that can withstand anything from earthquakes to high windstorms. Instead of simply stacking embankment stones or blocks, as is used customarily for holding back sloped sections of land, silo staves interlock, and are further held in place by huge steel coils, which are tightened by means of a type of turnbuckle that pulls the staves together.

Staves are held in place by means of metal coils and a special lug

(7) Two courses of Staves: Two courses of 30" silo staves bring the fish tank walls to a height of 5' which, when constructed with a diameter of 6', holds approximately 1050 gallons of water if filled to the rim. But since fish jump, it's recommended to drop the water level down a foot to 48", allowing for 900 gallons of water. The steel hoops around the perimeter of the stave wall are used to hold the silo staves in place while pulling them together when tightened with a lug, making the walls of the tank strong. The fish tank is now ready to be finished inside with a coating of concrete mortar to seal the joints and keep the water from leaking out.

The silo stave fish tank holds 1050 gallons of water when filled to the rim

(8) Coat the inner wall with concrete mortar: To seal the tank and prevent water leakage, coat the interior of the tank with concrete mortar. This can be trowelled on by an amateur as it doesn't have to be "perfect." However, the smoother the surface, the harder it is for aquatic plants like algae to cling to the tank wall. Contouring the concrete conical base of the tank when there is only one course of silo staves makes it easier to reach the center, where the concrete should be carefully spread to seal the ABS drain, which is closed by means of a faucet (see photo above).

A thick coat of concrete seals the tank from leakage

(9) Assemble the Raised Vegetable Bed Walls: Once the fish tank is complete, it's time to start on the inner and outer walls of the vegetable bed. This consists of a circular planting ring, 3' wide, that follows the inside perimeter of the BIODOME GARDEN, as shown on the diagram of the BIODOME GARDEN layout. As mentioned earlier, a second circular bed on the outside of the BIODOME GARDEN allows for tall vegetables such as corn and peas on vines, while also expanding the planting area beyond just what's inside, though the growing season for the vegetables outside of the BIODOME GARDEN will be shorter, depending on the region.

Assembling the silo stave walls is relatively easy. Silo staves are configured with pre-formed, cast concrete edges that are designed to nest together. But they also are able to stand alone while they are being arranged in a circle as shown above. Before setting up the silo staves, be sure to mark a circle for the wall to follow, using a circular guide and a can of white spray paint for ease in placing the staves, and to make sure the circle is in fact circular, or else the fiberglass dome will not fit properly, there will be gaps, and it will be difficult to attach.

Arranging the silo staves for the outer wall of the BIODOME GARDEN

(10) Rock Rodent Control: Placing 12" of river run rock at the bottom of the vegetable bed prevents rodents from burrowing up through the soil to eat roots and root crops. Some greenhouse builders use mesh wire to prevent rodents from burrowing under to feed on plants, but the rock adds mass for holding in the heat throughout the seasons, and unlike mesh, will never break down over time. Well-composted, potting-type soil is then added to the circular bed and brought up to the rim of the concrete staves to allow for compacting after watering.

River run rock prevents rodents from burrowing up under the soil

(11) Assemble the Biofilter: The diagram below outlines the basic working of the biofilter. The container is a fifty gallon fiberglass drum, with a hole drilled in the center of the bottom, using a hole saw, and a 1-1/2" PVC fitting glued into the hole with PVC cement. This fitting connects to a valve that opens up to drain the sludge in the bottom of the biofilter directly into the compost bin below. The fiberglass container is fitted with wooden slatted trays made out of cedar, and the trays hold oyster shells. Water from the fish tank is pumped up and flows out of a line into the top of the biofilter, where it runs through the oyster shells and out of a PVC fitting in the side of the biofilter, about 6" off the bottom of the biofilter, and down a cedar trough that drains it back into the tank, aerating the water.

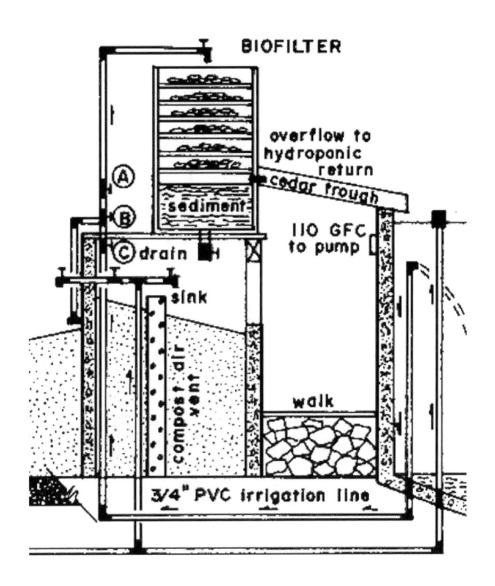

A fiberglass drum with oyster shells helps maintain a proper pH balance

(12) Water Timers Installed: Timing devices such as the ones in the photo above (round green objects), which can be purchased from home and garden centers, allows the perforated irrigation line in the vegetable bed to flow for a set amount of time and shut off automatically, restricting the amount of water used, while allowing the vegetable bed to be watered unattended. Use of a perforated irrigation line keeps water off the plant leaves, making for healthier, disease-free plants. To make this waterline, purchase a 20' section of 1" diameter PVC pipe and drill a series of holes, about 1/4" wide, and about 1" apart, along the length of it. Because of the larger holes, which allow water from the fish tank to pass through the pipes without clogging the line, the water will pass through rapidly, so you will need to monitor it the first few times you water in order to keep from flooding the bed. Soon you will know just how long to leave the water on. This irrigation ring lays on the surface along the outside perimeter of the vegetable bed.

(13) Construct the Hydroponic Troughs: The troughs in the photo below are constructed of 1"x8" cedar for the sides and bottoms. The "back board" is 5' long, with the troughs long enough to rest on the rim of the tank. The width of each trough is 8" to accommodate 8" wide cedar boards. For drainage, in the bottom of each trough, drill holes 2" wide and space them about 6" apart. Line each trough with fiberglass screening to keep the pea gravel or other planting medium from falling through the holes. Plants can be planted bare root in the gravel, and they do well, getting nutrients from the water from the fish tank as it's circulated through the biofilter and into the hydroponic troughs before returning to the fish tank. Alternately, soil can be added to the troughs, with wicking buried in the soil and dropping into the fish tank through the holes in the bottoms of the troughs--also lined with screening to prevent dirt from washing into the tank. Water from the tank makes its way up the wicking and keeps the soil moist. Both ways have been used successfully. Tomatoes and green peppers do especially well when grown hydroponically, but you can experiment with other vegetables to see what works for you in your regional environment.

Cedar is used to construct four hydroponic troughs in one unit

(14) ADD TOMATO CAGES: Tomato cages made from 1"x1" cedar can be added at the ends of the troughs. For ease of reaching and tending the other plants in the troughs, the cages are attached to the outside ends of the troughs with stainless steel screws. Tomatoes grow well bare-root in pea gravel, especially the small "bite-size" varieties. But pepper plants also grow well in cages. Be sure to complete the hydroponic troughs and set the unit in place over the fish tank before the dome goes on, or at least before the last section of the dome is fastened in place. Once the wind turbine is set on top and secured, it's a hassle to have to remove it, along with a panel of the dome, in order to get the hydroponic trough in.

Simple cages made from 1"x1" cedar are easy to build

(15) ADD A UTILITY SINK: With the fish tank complete, and the raised vegetable bed assembled, you can now add the utility sink and hook up the water lines. Although there are no photographs to guide you through the process of hooking up the water lines, anyone knowledgeable in working with PVC and ABS plastic pipes can do it easily by following the diagrams in this book. The sink in the photo below is a fiberglass utility sink, available for purchase at most home and garden centers. It's good to have a deep sink when washing vegetables, and the trimmings can be tossed directly into the compost bin, which is located right next to the sink. On the other side of the compost bin will be the worm bed, which is discussed in Chapter 5. If you look closely, you'll see a hose bib below the sink. This is handy for hosing the surfaces of the concrete tank and vegetable bed walls during extremely hot weather. It also adds moisture to the air during that time, while bringing down the temperature inside. Even then, it's a good idea to try to keep the water off the plants as that makes them more susceptible to plant diseases, which is why the irrigation ring is used. A soaker hose does the same thing, but it would clog up with sediment if used with water from the fish tank, so it should be connected to the faucet under the sink.

A deep utility sink means clean vegetables brought into the house

(16) GETTING A HEAD START: Meanwhile, if your fiberglass dome has not arrived--if ordered from a supplier who is making it when ordered--or if you are waiting for a geodesic dome kit to arrive, you can go ahead and start preparing your soil for the vegetable bed, or even planting your vegetables, if the bed is ready. Chapter 5 covers soil preparation, but if you don't want to bother with composting, and turning, and building up your own soil, a truckload of topsoil can be brought in and used for filling the vegetable bed. It will take approximately 10 yards of soil to fill the raised bed in a 16' diameter BIODOME GARDEN. Be sure to section off areas for a utility sink, as shown in the photo below (to the far left), as well as an area beside the sink to be used as a compost bin, and an area beside the compost bin for raising earthworms. These areas can be sectioned off using sheets of exterior plywood that are cut and fit to size and wedged in place. The compost bin will be below and behind the Biofilter so that sludge from the bottom of the biofilter can be drained directly into the compost bin.

Getting a head start in planting while waiting for the dome to arrive

(16) PREPARING FOR THE DOME: The fiberglass dome on the cover of the book was manufactured by a silo builder, and it came in eight interlocking panels that measured just over 6' each at the base. A similar dome can be purchased from one of the suppliers in the Appendix of this book. With whatever type of dome you purchase, you will receive instructions on how to assemble it. Or you can build your own geodesic dome. There are many resources available with directions on how to construct the framework for a geodesic dome. But whatever type of dome you decide on, you'll have to provide a means for attaching it to the outer wall of the BIDOME GARDEN. Local hardware stores or home and garden centers have numerous options that can be adapted. For the dome on the cover, heavy metal "straps" with a lineup of holes down the length of them were used. Shorter metal straps, positioned at right angles to the longer strap, and drilled with three holes, were used to connect the dome to the longer straps, with the center hole of the "T" bolted to a hole in the longer strap, and the two outer holes of the "T" connecting it to the dome like shown below. The photo shows how it was done with this BIODOME GARDEN, but you'll have to adapt your own means of fastening down the fiberglass dome on your BIODOME GARDEN, depending on how you construct your raised vegetable walls, and the kind of dome you purchase.

One means of attaching the dome to the wall of the BIODOME GARDEN

(17) ASSEMBLE THE DOME: Assembling the dome that is shown on the cover of this book was easy and only took two people to do it--one person to hold the pre-formed panels in place while the other person passed the 2" long bolts through pre-drilled holes in the fiberglass, and threaded on the nuts. If you purchase a similar type dome, DO NOT tighten down the nuts until all of the panels are up and in place or you will find yourself continually loosening nuts in order to adjust the panels. Once all of the panels are up, and in place, tighten the nuts in each bolt until firm, but not digging into the fiberglass. The ends of the bolts, which extend 2" inside the dome, are handy for using as hooks for hanging planter boxes up under the dome. The opening in the fiberglass panel below is one of three vents, that remain open during the summer months. Sliding, unhinged covers, as shown in a photo below, cover the vent openings during the cold winter months.

Sections of the dome laid out in preparation for assembling

The photo below shows the many features of the BIODOME GARDEN: a deep utility sink, which is set into the vegetable bed area and shown at the far right of the photo, a fish tank in the center of the BIODOME GARDEN, hydroponic troughs that rest on top of the fish tank, the Biofilter, which is shown in the photo, to the upper left of the fish tank, large vent openings in the fiberglass dome, and the raised, circular vegetable bed. A compost bin is located next to the sink and directly beneath the Biofilter, and an earthworm bin is located next to the compost bin. There will also be mushroom flats in the open area beneath the sink, and this is discussed further in Chapter 9.

Two people assembling the dome on the BIODOME GARDEN on the cover

The dome is assembled and ready for the wind turbine

(18) ATTACH THE WIND TURBINE: This is the final step. The fiberglass panels do not come to peaks at top, but rather are curved in arcs so that when the panels are fitted, and the tops come together, an open circle is formed that allows the "skirt" of the wind turbine to drop through. The wind turbine is also fitted into a round fiberglass "disk" about 18" in diameter, as shown in the photo below, and when the unit (the wind turbine and the fiberglass disk) is placed on top of the dome, it acts like a giant washer to strengthen and reinforce the area where the wind turbine sits. Be sure to purchase a very good-quality wind turbine as this will be your sole means of ventilation, and you'll want a turbine that will catch the slightest breeze and also spin rapidly as the hot air rises to the peak of the dome, where it is exhausted quickly and efficiently. During winter months you will need to place a long section of 1"x1" cedar (or an old broom handle) up into the base of the wind turbine to keep it from spinning, or it will remove the warm air inside.

The wind turbine on top eliminates the need for an electrical ventilation system

(19) SLIP THE SIDE VENT COVERS IN PLACE: Good ventilation is extremely important for proper temperature control. As the wind turbine continues to capture the prevailing summer breeze, the three large air vents (or openings) in the sides of three of the fiberglass dome panels promote a natural flow of air from a low entry and upward to a high exit through the wind turbine. The side vents in the fiberglass dome on the cover of the book were designed so that large, pre-formed, fiberglass covers could slip into place at the top of each opening, without the use of hardware, and remain in the open position on their own. By lifting slightly and pulling forward, the covers can be lowered to completely close the vent opening by tucking under a bottom pre-formed flange as shown in the photos below. This is a unique design that can be incorporated into a custom-built dome and fabricated by a regional fiberglass merchant.

A unique design enables the side vents to operate without hardware

PREPARING THE VEGETABLE BED

Building a Potting Soil Bed

The primary purpose of a raised bed is to provide better garden drainage and greater soil warmth for early plantings. Some other advantages are higher yields from a small area, and the tendency of some vegetables planted in raised beds to mature earlier. But a raised bed is only as good as the soil it contains. Soil is a living bio-entity teeming with millions of microorganisms that include algae, fungi, protozoa, bacteria and earthworms, and these organisms need organic matter to thrive and survive. So one of the most important aspects of BIODOME GARDENING is building your soil. Its power to sustain healthy plant growth is dependent on how you prepare and maintain it. You can either begin well ahead of the construction of your BIODOME GARDEN by starting a compost bin, or you can have a load of topsoil brought in, which runs the chance of introducing perennial weeds. The most practical choice is a combination of the two: haul in topsoil for the bottom 2' of your raised vegetable bed, and fill the top 6" with rich, crumbly soil prepared from compost in your own compost bin. In any event, any serious gardener will tell you that for an organic garden to be successful, compost is the key.

(1) BUILD A COMPOST BIN: Ultimately you'll have a compost bin inside your BIODOME GARDEN, where you can deposit plant clippings, worm castings, and other organic matter, but at this point in your project you'll have to begin building your soil in a soil bin. There are several ways you can prepare a compost bin. An easy way is to nail together four 2"x12"x14' boards as a framework to hold the soil. Alternately, you can purchase a length of woven wire about 12' feet long and 4' high and form it into a circle, while letting the wire overlap for strength and ease of wiring the ends together. With the wire bin, once it is full and starting to "cook," the wire can be removed and set beside the composting pile, and the bin filled again. A bin made with (4) 2"x12"x14' boards is large enough that you can have several compost piles cooking at the same time.

(2) WHAT TO PUT IN THE BIN: Anything that will rot will compost, so the list of what you can toss onto the compost heap is endless. It can be fruit and vegetable peelings, coffee grounds and tea bags, leaves, grass clippings, egg shells, chicken and fish bones--whatever you'd ordinarily grind up in the disposer. If you keep a small plastic bucket handy in the kitchen, you can collect scraps daily and toss them into the compost. Shredded paper and newspapers, soft prunings, grass clippings and old cut flowers, leaves, wood ash and droppings from pet cages, all make good compost. Other organic products that are readily accessible and inexpensive, and which you can haul in, are sawdust, bark chips, pole peelings, and chipped pruning materials.

(3) MANURE FOR NITROGEN: Nitrogen is needed for breaking down organic matter, and manure is an excellent source of nitrogen. Manure mixed with straw can be found at any horse farm or stables, and is usually free for the hauling. This can be spaded throughout the organic mix. Additional leaves, sawdust, grass, clippings, kitchen waste and manure can be layered as they become available. You can also add the top soil that was removed when you prepared the gravel base for the BIODOME GARDEN. This will create a soil-organic mix sufficient for adequate rooting of most vegetable plants.

(4) WHAT NOT TO PUT IN THE BIN: Some decomposable items attract vermin and should be avoided, such as meat and cooked foods, unless buried well into the compost pile. Waste from the cat box, or what's scooped up from the dog yard is questionable due to the risk of spreading disease. But droppings from rabbits and hamsters and caged birds work well, acting as compost accelerators. But the key to good composting is variety. Woody prunings take a long time to break down, kitchen scraps attract flies if they make up the bulk of the compost, and grass clippings alone can start to smell as they break down, so the trick is to layer a variety of organic material.

(5) **BUILDING THE COMPOST MIX**: Begin the process by putting a 4"-5" layer of organic matter into the bin. Next, toss vegetable scraps, egg shells and other waste from the kitchen on top. Continue alternating with organic matter from outside, and scraps from the kitchen, until your bin is full. Because the process is slow, taking up to a year for the compost to "cook," and ultimately turn into the wonderful, crumbly, organic soil referred to by farmers as "black gold", you might want to build several compost bins if you have the space.

(6) **KEEP THE MIX BALANCED**: If you add too much kitchen waste to your compost bin, and not enough dried materials to offset the mix, the rotting scraps will attract flies, which are not among the beneficial bugs that you want. The success of your end product depends on the ratio of nitrogen to carbon, with a sizeable amount of oxygen. Materials high in carbon include dried grass clippings, dried leaves, dried manure and sawdust. Materials high in nitrogen include fresh grass clippings, and kitchen waste that is still green and moist, like the leftovers from salads. To keep the compost balanced, add proportionate amounts of both dried and fresh materials. A proper balance will boost the breakdown of kitchen scraps into soil, promote odorless decay, and absorb excess moisture, while also eliminating problems with flies that are attracted to the rotting scraps.

(7) **TURN THE PILE PERIODICALLY**: It's also important to turn the contents of the heap periodically to aerate it and to inject oxygen into it. When the "tossings" in the compost bin are no longer recognizable, and have broken down into a pulverable mixture, it's ready to mix with the topsoil that will go into the vegetable bed. The added organic matter will boost fertility, aiding plants in building resistance to insect attack and disease, while improving the structure of the soil.

An ideal mix for filling the vegetable bed is topsoil "topped" with seasoned compost

(8) **FILL IN THE BED**: As mentioned earlier, be sure to shovel the soil into the vegetable bed before the dome is put on or it will be extremely difficult, and very time consuming, to have to shovel it through the vent windows. As it is, a lot of soil will have to be moved just to fill the 3' wide vegetable planting ring to a depth of 30". Pile in the soil right up to the rim of the inner silo stave wall because it will settle down when watered, and more soil will have to be added. Save your best soil from your compost bin until the vegetable bed has been well-watered, several times, then use to make up the top 6".

(9) **CHECK FOR pH**: It's a good idea to test your soil's pH periodically to make sure it isn't too acid or too alkaline. Easy-to-use test kits are available from your local cooperative extension, or they can be purchased from garden centers. The test is measured on a scale of 1.0 to 14.0, the low end being acidic, and the high end being alkaline, with 7.0 being neutral. Most plants do best on a slightly acidic soil of about 6.5. If too acid, lime can be mixed in at a rate of about 5 pounds of lime per 100 square feet of soil surface (which is the approximate soil surface of the vegetable bed in the BIODOME GARDEN). Lime is absorbed slowly, so it should be mixed in well before planting, and usually not more than every three years. If the soil is too alkaline, you can add sulfur to lower the pH. Add about 1-1/2 pounds of sulfur per 100 square feet of soil surface. The soil test will also recommend other micronutrients, and it's a good idea to add them at that time.

(10) MULCHING: Conditions inside the BIODOME GARDEN are naturally more humidified than with an outside garden, but it's still a good idea to use some mulch to hold in moisture. Mushroom compost is one of the best mulches because not only does it help hold in moisture, but it's also rich in nutrients. Directions for raising mushrooms are covered in Chapter 9. About a 1"-2" layer works well. Wood chips can also be used, but you should allow them to compost for a minimum of six months or they may deplete the soil of nitrogen.

EARTHWORMS FOR HEALTHY SOIL AND FISH FOOD

Preparing an earthworm bed can give you a supply of rich, organic matter loaded with nitrogen and other nutrients for building up the soil in your compost bin. A worm bed can easily be constructed, much the same as the wooden compost bin but smaller, and placed beside the compost bin, where "castings" from the worm bed can be added to the compost whenever it becomes available. But for the purpose of this book, keeping and maintaining earthworms will be discussed in regards to conditions inside the BIODOME GARDEN, and you can apply it to an outside earthworm bed.

Redworms are preferable to "wigglers"

(1) LOCATING THE WORM BED: Because of the space restrictions in the BIODOME GARDEN, a section of the vegetable bed, divided off as a worm bed about 3' feet wide, will give you a sufficient quantity of earthworms for all your BIODOME GARDEN needs. Section off the worm bed with untreated plywood, and place it next to the compost bin so that later, the old soil from the worm bed, with it's high-nutrient castings, can be removed and dumped directly into the compost bin.

(2) PREPARE THE BED: The depth of the worm bed will be the depth of the raised garden. Because the food for the worms is always placed on top of the bed, the worms will not burrow down very deep into the bed. Fill the worm bed with the same soil you will use in the vegetable bed, but leave 6" of space on top that can be filled with peat moss, which can be purchased in bags from home and garden centers. Once you have added the peat moss, water the bed to keep the peat moist, but not flooded. The bed is now ready for worms.

(3) INTRODUCE THE EARTHWORMS: These can be purchased from local bait shops that sell fishing tackle and gear. Avoid buying "wigglers" because they take more care. Redworms are preferable. For a worm bed the size that will be in the BIODOME GARDEN, which is around 3' x 3,' purchase about 200 earthworms. Turn them into the bed and they will find their way into the peat moss.

(4) KEEP IT MOIST: Earthworms are easy keepers, as long as they have a moist environment, so be sure to keep the worm beds damp all the time. If the weather becomes hot and dry, it's important to water the worm bed daily. But don't flood the bed. On the other hand, if the temperature is too cold, the worms will not survive. In very cold weather cover the bed with a scrap of carpet, or several burlap feed bags, or other heavy material to keep the worms warm. They will burrow down into the soil, where it's warmer, but they still need to come to the surface to feed.

(5) BED MAINTENANCE: The enclosed environment of the BIODOME GARDEN with the diffused dome above is conducive to retaining moisture, so the beds will not dry out as quickly as they would in an outside environment during warm weather, but they will still dry out. Just don't overwater, allowing the beds to flood.

(4) FEEDING THE WORMS: You can purchase Purina Worm chow from local garden stores. This comes in powder form and is easy to apply. But you can supplement this by sprinkling coffee grounds mixed with ground oatmeal over the top of the worm bed a few times a week. Simply coat the top of the worm bed with whatever food you choose and the worms will come to the surface. In minutes, the food will be gone. Just don't overfeed. Worms should be fed daily, but they should clean up all the food daily too, to keep it from molding.

(5) **RAPID REPRODUCTION**: If done properly, the worms should start reproducing rapidly, and soon you can begin distributing the overflow throughout the vegetable beds so that they can burrow down into the soil, aerating it while depositing castings. Before long, you will have an overabundance of worms and you can start feeding them to the fish.

(6) **MAINTAINING THE PEAT**: As the peat moss level in the worm bed goes down, replace it with fresh peat by adding it to the top 6" of the bed. The fresh peat does not need to be mixed with the old.

(7) **USING CASTINGS FOR COMPOST**: In a few months you can start rotating the old soil with its worm castings, into the compost bin, for turning it into the vegetable beds between crops. To separate the worms from the old soil, use a small, short-handled rake and sift through the soil to lift out the worms, which you can dump on the opposite side of the worm bed. Remove the worm-free soil and toss it into the compost bin. Replace the dirt that was removed with fresh peat moss, and you're ready to start the cycle over again. With this method you will produce chemical-free soil with an abundance of nutrients for supporting healthy plants.

(8) **WATERING**: Adequate irrigation is important with raised beds because the soil warms early in the season, and plant growth takes moisture from the soil rapidly. However, overwatering can also kill plants by causing little or no root growth, bacterial and fungal diseases, and low fertility level. If choosing between the options of watering heavily and less frequently, and watering lightly and more frequently, lighter watering is the better choice. But the water needs of plants also change seasonally. During the summer months it's best to water late in the day, when the sun's still high and it will be several hours before darkness. This is not the case with an outside garden, where early morning watering is preferable because it gives the leaves time to dry out before nightfall. But with the use of the irrigation ring for watering, the leaves of plants growing inside the BIODOME GARDEN

are not subjected moisture, only the roots. But in winter, when the days are short and the temperature is cold, watering should be cut way back. Grow lights are also advised to help offset the lower levels of light.

(9) GOOD DRAINAGE: Lastly, the vegetable bed should also be flat on top to prevent irrigation water from running off rather than soaking in. Because loam soils drain and warm up quickly, they are excellent for raised beds. But the benefit of planting your garden in raised beds, and within an ecologically-balanced environment such as the BIODOME GARDEN is an abundance of fresh, nutritious vegetables.

Conditions inside the BIODOME GARDEN are ideal for plant growth

6 UTILIZING THE WATER TANK

Fish? Or a hot tub surrounded by flowers?

Imagine a cold, gray, winter day where the ground is covered with snow, and the birds are silent, and all the sounds of summer--crickets, tree frogs, the buzz of bees--have died. But inside your BIODOME GARDEN, a lush, green, all-season environment of herbs and ornamentals, and maybe a few hardy flowers raise their colorful heads toward your grow lights above. And you immerse yourself in the comfortable warmth of a hot tub and sit back and just relax and unwind from a busy day. Or it's early morning, and you're preparing for the day ahead. Pampering yourself also promotes a healthful lifestyle. This scenario is especially appealing if you imagine yourself relaxing in a hot tub located in a BIODOME GARDEN ROOM, which is located just off the family room or master bedroom, where it's only a few steps away from hot-tubbing bliss. There are no rules in the book that say you have to raise organic vegetables and maintain them with the water from raising fish. A hot tub surrounded by ornamental plants is okay. But if you're a dyed-in-the-wool, back-to-the-lander, you will want fish. Some do well in the enclosed environment of a fish tank, others not so well. Through experimentation, and the accessibility of aquatic animals and fish, you can determine which animals survive and thrive in your climate zone and environment. Some freshwater varieties to try are included.

Stocking the tank with aquatic animals

(1) **FRESHWATER FISH**: Asian markets customarily have large tanks in the store with lobsters and other aquatic animals for sale. The internet is also a good source for locating aquatic animals for purchase. These aquatic animals can include, but are not limited to, the following:

a) **GOLDFISH**: There are many different varieties of goldfish, and most are suitable for tank conditions. They are bright in color, so they are easily spotted, and they adapt readily to conditions. They also breed easily, producing lots of fry. Varieties include the *Comet*, which is a very hardy type with a long single tail fin, and which can reach 12-14 inches. Colorful beneath the surface of the water, they are a bright, metallic orange with white spots. Another variety worth considering is the *Common Goldfish*, which is usually a solid, bright orange in color, and which can also reach 12-14 inches. The *Fantail Goldfish* is larger around, taking on a kind of egg shape. It's long tail is split into two lobes, making it appear flowing. Reaching up to 14 inches, *Fantails* are also very hardy, their coloring a bright metallic orange with some mottling in black and pale orange. The *Shubunkin*, with a somewhat flowing tail, looks similar to a *Comet*, with coloring ranging from oranges to golds to reds, blacks and whites in calico patterns. The *Shubunkin* is shorter than the others, but thicker around, growing to about 10 inches.

Blushing Apricot goldfish are beautiful additions to a tank

b) JAPANESE KOI: Japanese Koi, cousins of the Goldfish, are beautiful and colorful, with long flowing tails. It is said that they can live for two-hundred years, but typically, in a pond, they live for twenty-five to forty years, so if you decide to stock your tank with pet fish, they may be with you for a very long time. What's fun about having Koi is that they can be tamed to eat out of your hand. Pelleted food is ideal for this, and it can supplement the natural food they get in the tank. Although not especially tasty, Koi adapt well to a tank environment, and are ideal for adding nutrients to the water, which in turn aids in plant growth when vegetables are irrigated with the water from the fish tank. However, large Koi need approximately 200 gallons of water per fish, so that has to be taken into account. One nice variety to consider is the *Butterfly Koi*, which has an extremely long and flowing split-fin tail, and varied coloring, some in metallic white, others in mixed shades of gold, orange, black and white. *Butterfly Koi,* also known as *"fancy-tail,"* like other koi, can reach lengths of about 14 to 16 inches.

A great-granddaddy tri-color Koi about 16" long

Another beautiful variety of Koi is the Yellow Koi. What's nice about this particular variety is that their bright yellow coloring makes them easy to spot in the tank, even when swimming close to the bottom. They love to swim in schools though, so plan to purchase several.

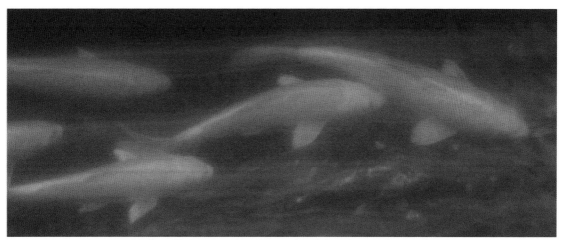
Yellow Koi swimming in a school brighten the tank

c) CATFISH: Catfish are hardy, bottom feeders that help keep the tank from getting murky. However, the larger varieties like the Channel Catfish will eat whatever they can fit in their mouths, and they have voracious appetites for live fish, so unless you are interested in stocking your fish tank with only Channel Catfish, you might want to consider a smaller variety like the Madtom Catfish. Although some of this variety have fancy coloration, most are just plain brown. This fish grows to about 6" long in large aquariums so they pose little threat to other fish in the tank. Like most catfish, they have whiskery faces and sharp spines on their dorsal fins. They're also bottom feeders that scavenge for "leftovers" on the bottom of the tank. Don't overstock. Two in a tank this size are enough.

Catfish are good tank fish for keeping the bottom clean

59

d) MOSQUITO FISH: These small fish are one of the most effective means of controlling mosquitoes in the tank. They range from one to two inches, and are related to the guppy. They co-exist with Koi, goldfish and other pond fish, and each fish eats up to 300 mosquito larvae and pupae per day. They are hardy and can survive in water temperatures from 30 to 100 degrees. They also breed readily, so their fry are food for the larger fish in the tank. Substitutes are minnows, shiners or darters.

Mosquito Fish consume copious quantities of mosquito larvae daily

e) MINNOWS: Minnows are traditionally sold as bait for fishermen, and as feeder fish in aquarium stores. Bait minnows are olive-brown to black, but the mutant Rosy Red minnow was developed for both fishermen and aquarium owners to be more visible, ranging in tones from "rosy red" to light orange in color, which makes then a nice fish for the tank.

Rosy Red Minnows are often called "tuffies" when sold as "feeder fish"

f) TADPOLES: The larger fish will keep the tadpole population manageable, and in turn, frogs in the BIODOME GARDEN will spawn plenty of tadpoles for the fish to eat. More about tadpoles later in the chapter.

(2) SNAILS AND CRUSTACEANS: This group includes clams and mussels of fresh water varieties, and snails, crayfish and lobsters. Bivalves feed on microscopic plants and animals, while their young provide food for other aquatic animals. Many can be purchased live from Asian fish markets.

a) CRAYFISH: Crayfish, a freshwater variant of the lobster, are good for keeping the tank clean. Once introduced, they can be found scavenging for small fish, plant debris, water insects, snails, clams, worms and larvae. They have good eyesight and can move their eyes independently from one another. These crustaceans reach adult size in about four years, and they have a lifespan of 20 to 30 years. After molting, they eat their own skeletons to replace the calcium and phosphates contained in them and lost during molting. During breeding season, the males become aggressive and may lose a leg or claw during a fight, but it will slowly grow back. However, introducing crayfish means sacrificing plants as the crayfish will eat them.

Crayfish can live for 20 to 30 years

b) NERITE SNAILS: These snails are very hardy, being able to live in water temperatures that range between 40 and 90 degrees. They are scavengers that not only control the growth of algae, but also clean excess food and debris from the walls and bottom of the tank. They lay eggs, but the eggs won't hatch unless the water is brackish, so they will not populate the tank. However, don't include Koi with snails as the Koi will suck the snails out of their shells. Adult snails live about 1 year.

61

Algae-eating Nerite snails help clean the tank

c) **BLUE KNIGHT LOBSTERS**: These attain lengths of up to 12". Their colors vary from a brilliant blue to a bluish brown, and they have small claws for their size. They are easy to care for and breed readily in captivity, producing eggs that hatch in 21 days. However, the fry need to be removed to separate buckets of water to prevent them from killing and eating each other. The fry can be fed flake or pellet food from a fish supply until they are big enough to return to the tank. Blue Knights are omnivorous scavengers, eating food and plant debris that settles to the bottom of the tank. They thrive in water between 68-85 degrees, but they are territorial and need at least 50 gallons of water each. Also include plenty of cover such as plants, where they can hide.

Blue Knight Lobsters cleaning the tank by scavenging

62

ESTABLISHING A COLONY OF FROGS AND TOADS

Frogs and toads eat 3 times their weight in bugs per night

WHY ESTABLISH FROGS AND TOADS? For starters, a single frog or toad can consume up to three times it's body weight in ants, squash bugs, cucumber and potato beetles, flies, earwigs, grasshoppers, crickets, pillbugs and cutworms—*every day*. In fact, toads and frogs are the *only* beneficial creatures that eat cucumber beetles, which are the bad bugs that cause cucumbers to be bitter by feeding on cucumber vines. Frogs and toads also eat slugs, but if you have a big slug problem and need to put out slug bait, iron phosphate baits are safe to use around toads and frogs.

START WITH TADPOLES: Tadpoles do well in the enclosed environment of the fish tank, and they also help rid the water of algae. In addition to that, they are a good source of food for the fish. Like other small aquatic animals, they will need a place to hide, so including floating aquatic plants is important for their survival. Tadpoles also need relatively fresh water, so the biofilter system is ideal for keeping the water at a level of clarity that allows the tadpoles to thrive and change into frogs.

Tadpoles help rid the water of algae

WHERE TO GET TADPOLES: Tadpoles are good to include in your tank as fish food if you have Koi, or as a means of producing frogs for bug control in your BIODOME GARDEN. They are easy to obtain. Most farm ponds with good frog populations have a ready supply that can be caught with a dip net and a bucket. But keep in mind that if you intend to include tadpoles in your tank for anything other than fish food, you'll need to reconsider having Koi since Koi will eat about anything in the tank, including bugs, algae, plants and baby fish. But if you do decide you want Koi too, include only Koi of a size that is not a threat to tadpoles. At least not for a while. Bullfrog tadpoles are bigger than regular tadpoles, but once they become bull frogs they'll eat everything Koi would, including tadpoles.

FEEDING TADPOLES: One of their favorite foods is lettuce. To prepare it for them, boil a bunch for 10-15 minutes, then chop it up and freeze it in ice trays. You can drop a cube into the tank every few days. Tadpoles and other aquatic animals will gobble it up quickly. But tadpoles also love aphids, so if you find aphids on your vegetables you can hand pick them and drop them into the fish tank and the tadpoles will have a feast.

FROM TADPOLE TO FROGLET: Tadpoles start out as fish-like creatures with fins, living underwater and breathing through gills. Through a gradual process of growth, they acquire legs and lose their tail, until they become four-legged, air breathing creatures at full development. The length of time it takes for a tadpole to develop into a frog or a toad depends on several factors, one being the species the tadpole came from. Some tadpoles become frogs or toads in as little as six to nine weeks while others can take as long as eight months. However, if the eggs were laid at the end of the summer, when the temperature begins to fall and the water in the tank is cooler, the tadpoles may remain tadpoles until spring.

FROGLETS AND TOADLETS APPEAR: All surviving tadpoles eventually develop legs and need to have something to sit on, and to eventually be able to get out of the tank. To aid them in this, you can include floating water lilies since young frogs like to sit on the lilies' network of branches and large flat leaves. Young tree frogs can climb up the side of the tank, but ground-dwelling frogs will need a rough sloping surface. For this you can also build a small cedar platform and rig it so it's sitting on the water next to the side of the tank where they hop to the rim, and from there, a short leap to the vegetable bed. Young frogs and toads like to hide under plants and rocks when they can, and if conditions are right, they will establish a permanent breeding ground in the BIODOME GARDEN where they can help rid the vegetable beds of plant-eating insects. Be sure to place a couple of terra cotta planting pots on their sides on the north side of the structure to create a cool, damp, dark cavern for them to hide in during the day.

FEEDING YOUNG FROGS AND TOADS: If the frogs and toads aren't big enough to eat larger insect pests like crickets, and there aren't enough smaller insects in your garden to feed them, you can supplement them with bloodworms. These can be purchased live from pet stores that sell fish. Place a few worms in a small, shallow container like the lid of a jar, with some tank water added, and the young frogs and toads will find them. You can also drop some directly into the water.

EGGS MEAN THAT FROGS AND TOADS ARE ESTABLISHED: If you see clusters or strings of round, jelly-like pearls with black dots in the center, it's likely your frogs or toads have returned to the tank to lay their eggs, and the cycle is complete. Toad eggs show up in the water as a string of eggs, while frog eggs comes in clusters. However toad and frog tadpoles grow up in a similar way. The main differences between the two is that toad tadpoles are darker, sometimes black, and smaller than frog tadpoles.

FISH EAT TADPOLES: Frogs and toads are great for controlling insects in your BIODOME GARDEN, and fun to raise from tadpole to froglet to fully-matured frog, but if you have large fish in your tank, they'll eat the frogspawn and tadpoles. Aquatic plants with tangles of greenery for the tadpoles to hide in, will help, but the tads will still be a target for big-mouth fish whenever they venture out from their hiding places. So if you want a healthy population of frogs, populate your tank with small fish.

WATER DEPTH: Frogs need deep water for hibernating, and shallow water for spawning. Obviously the tank can't accommodate the shallowness, so you will have to provide something for the young frogs to crawl out onto when their legs are formed. Small floating slabs of cedar, or large flat Lily pads work well, and later, the adult frogs and toads can spawn among the pads and root system.

Most of the year frogs and toads are on land feeding

DENSE VEGETATION: Frogs and toads only spend some of their time in the water, but for most of the year, they're on land feeding. They like cool, damp places, so they will seek out the coolness of the north side of the BIODOME GARDEN, and many will leave if it gets too hot. But in time, a new population will crawl out of the tank to feed on garden pests.

Stocking the tank with aquatic plants

WHY ADD PLANTS? If you have fish, plants provide them with food, shade and places to hide. But the main reason to include plants is that they use up nutrients that algae needs to grow, so they aid in reducing algae in the water. Without plants, algae tends to take over since algae and plants compete for nutrients in the water. By converting fish waste into food, plants in turn filter the water. Aquatic plants also provide spawning habitat while offering places for aquatic animals to hide, especially the small, young and vulnerable. Be aware that some pond plants, like water hyacinths, are illegal in some states because if they are introduced into rivers or lakes they multiply rapidly and can hurt the ecosystem, so you may be restricted in purchasing these and certain others, depending on where you live. The plants are divided into flaoting plants and submerged plants.

OXYGENATOR PLANTS: Certain aquatic plants add oxygen to the water, which is essential for raising fish, by converting carbon dioxide into oxygen. During the day, plants breathe in carbon dioxide and release oxygen. At night, they take in oxygen and release carbon dioxide. Plants use carbon dioxide for photosynthesis and to produce energy. Aquatic plants also consume nitrates and phosphates that build up in the water. By absorbing minerals and carbon dioxide in the water, the foliage of aquatic plants starve algae. Numerous pond plants are available for purchase from local and online suppliers. The list is too long to include in this book, so only a few of the known hardier varieties will be included. These are plants that can withstand cold climates, although they are not as colorful as the tropical varieties. But for those living in the warm climates, there are more options.

REMINDER: If you're purchasing plants from an online supplier, you'll have to check with your state agents to see if there are any restrictions. There should be no problem if you purchase from a local pond supplier.

SUBMERGED OXYGENATOR PLANTS: These water plants continuously supplement the water with oxygen, which is essential in a fish tank. They are so effective that bubbles of oxygen can be observed coming from their leaves. Like floating plants, submerged plants absorb nitrates and phosphates in the water, depriving algae of what it needs to survive. Submerged plants also provide spawning media for fish, frogs, and snails. About six to ten plants, with their roots planted in pea gravel contained in submersible baskets, are adequate for the fish tank. To make it easy to clean the tank it's best not to put submerged plants in soil in pots, as is the method with outdoor ponds. Instead, purchase underwater baskets and put pea gravel in them. After clumping the roots in bunches, gently cover them with gravel then lower the basket into the tank. The roots will feed on the nutrients in the water, especially from fish waste. Adding submerged plants also gives small aquatic animals a place to hide.

1) **ELODEA:** This plant is an outstanding oxygenator, as well as a good consumer of nitrates in the water. It's also a good indicator of the quality of the water because in hard water, calcium deposits will cover it. It develops thickets in the bottom of the tank where aquatic animals can hide, while on the surface, white flowers can bloom against its dark green leaves throughout the summer months.

Baskets with pea gravel hold plant roots at the bottom of the tank

2) **HORNWORT:** This beautiful plant provides Koi and other egg-scattering fish a good spawning medium as well as a place for fish fry to hide. It grows free-floating and spends it's life completely submersed. Because it doesn't root, it derives all of its nutrients from the water, so it's useful in keeping the water free of excess algae.

3) **WATER LILIES:** These hardy plants are good oxygenators and are easy to maintain. Frogs like to sit on their tough, flat leaves, which encourages breeding and maintenance of tadpoles as fish food.

White Lily

Red Lily

FLOATING OXYGENATOR PLANTS: These low-maintenance, hardy plants are easy to introduce into your fish tank. Just lay them in the water and you're done. Floating plants should cover about sixty percent of the surface of the water for good balance. They help keep the water cool in the summer while also helping to control the growth of algae.

1) **WATER HYACINTH:** The water hyacinth, with its beautiful purple bloom, is a nice choice for the fish tank. It floats on the surface, is a prolific grower, and helps keep the water oxygenated. Many cities use water hyacinths in their water treatment plants to pre-filter the waste water. But they are also a favorite food of Koi, who like to nibble on their root tips, so you will have to replace them periodically. After a while the root masses will become entangled and should be pulled apart to encourage new growth. Of the hyacinths, Jumbo Water Hyacinths are probably the most prolific growers, so they are especially helpful in keeping the pond water clear, and they produce beautiful flowers.

2) **MINIATURE WATER HYACINTH:** This pretty hyacinth is almost identical to the traditional water hyacinth except that it's much smaller, about half the size, so it's good for smaller areas like the fish tank. It is also more tolerant of cold than the larger variety.

Water Hyacinths

Miniature Water Hyacinth

3) **WATER LETTUCE:** These plants, with their masses of roots that extend into the water are great water filtration aids. Their velvety leaves spread and form rosettes on the water surface, making them a favorite among pond owners. They also produce runners that spread in all directions, forming colonies wherever they can remain undisturbed.

4) FOUR-LEAF CLOVER: These low-maintenance plants are easy to grow, and they float on the surface as the trailing vines spread, making them great for surface coverage.

Water Lettuce

Four-Leaf Clover

5) FROGBIT: These easy growers spread quickly, also making them great plants for surface coverage. Their heart-shaped leaves are only a few inches around, resembling miniature water lilies.

6) WATER-SENSITIVE PLANT: This small-leafed water plant with it's yellow, puffball-like flowers, floats on the surface of the water by means of swollen, air-filled sections of the stems. When their small leaves are touched they snap shut, but they open again in minutes. At night, or when the weather's cool, the leaves also close.

Frogbit

Water-Sensitive Plant

7) DUCKWEED: This plant, with its small, bright-green leaves, is excellent for feeding herbivorous fish. The leaves use up free nutrients in the water, and they vary in size according to nutrient supply. Under proper conditions, reproduction, which is by budding, can be very rapid.

8) WATERMEAL: Watermeal is the smallest flowering water plant, although it blooms only rarely. But its tiny leaves make it an excellent food for herbaceous fish. It also forms dense colonies just below the surface in which small aquatic animals can hide.

70

7 INCLUDING HYDROPONICS

Why include hydroponics?

That's simple. Instead of soil, hydroponic gardening uses nutrient-rich solution, and with 900 gallons of the stuff continually circulating from the fish tank to the biofilter, and back to the fish tank, it would be a shame not to capitalize on this. And all of this with little or no labor, once the plants are growing. But utilizing the nutrient-rich water is only one of the many advantages of hydroponic gardening.

Not only is hydroponic gardening an environmentally-friendly way to garden, but plants tend to be healthier because they grow in a pest-free medium and don't have to contend with organisms in the soil that often attack their roots. They also grow thirty to fifty percent faster than plants grown in soil, because in soil, plants must grow large root systems in order to search for food and water. But in hydroponics, nutrients go directly to the roots so the plants don't have to compete with other plants, as they would if growing in soil, and they can put their energy into growing the part above the surface. Also, with smaller root systems, plants can be grown close together. In general, hydroponic systems require about eighty percent less space to produce the same quantity of vegetables as plants grown in soil. In addition, hydroponically-grown plants are healthier and more vigorous, and they have less problem with funguses, bug infestation, and plant disease. But there's one last advantage. There's very little labor involved. No weeding. No soil maintenance. No digging. And no worry about under-watering or over-watering. Just get those roots established in your planting medium, and then go tend to the rest of the plants in your BIODOME GARDEN and leave the hydroponics alone. It's also been shown that if two genetically identical plants are grown using soil for one, and hydroponics for the other, the one using hydroponics will grow faster, be hardier and healthier, and give a higher yield, which is why hydroponics are being adapted for commercial food production around the world.

(1) **RECOVERY AND NON-RECOVERY HYDROPONIC SYSTEMS:** Hydroponic systems are classified as passive or active, recovery or non-recovery. A recovery system re-circulates the nutrient solution so that it is used again, while a non-recovery system applies the nutrient solution to the growing medium as it passes through only once, at which time the solution is disposed of. The BIODOME GARDEN uses a recovery system by re-circulating the water from the fish tank, through the Biofilter, into the hydroponic troughs, and back into the fish tank, where nutrients are continuously being added to the water by the aquatic animals in the tank.

(2) **ACTIVE VERSUS PASSIVE SYSTEMS:** Hydroponic garden systems are characterized as active or passive, both systems adaptable for use in the BIODOME GARDEN, and both having been used successfully.

a) **ACTIVE HYDROPONIC SYSTEM:** An active system "actively" moves the nutrient solution to the plant roots by use of a pump. With the BIODOME GARDEN, troughs are constructed as described in Chapter 4 (page 39), with 2" holes in the bottom of the troughs, as shown in the photo below, for the water to run out. The fish and other aquatic animals provide the nutrients in the hydroponic solution, and plants absorb the nutrients as the water passes over the roots.

An active system where water flows through the troughs past the roots

b) PASSIVE HYDROPONIC SYSTEM: This system uses capillary action to deliver the nutrient solution to the plant roots. With the BIODOME GARDEN, this is done by setting up a wicking system, as shown in the photo below, where the plants are rooted in a medium such as vermiculite, perlite or sand, with wicking buried in the medium and dropping through the holes in the bottom of the hydroponic troughs, and into the fish tank. Water from the fish tank travels up the wicks through capillary action, and the medium in the troughs holds the moisture while the roots absorb nutrients from it. A pump is not needed for a passive system, but since a pump is already in use in the fish tank, an active system would be the best choice since passive systems tend to not supply enough oxygen to the root system for optimum growth rates.

73

Passive hydroponic system using wicking to deliver the nutrient solution

(3) THE WICK SYSTEM VERSUS THE EBB-AND-FLOW SYSTEM: Both systems have been used successfully in the BIODOME GARDEN so the following should help you decide which way works best for your conditions. Removing pea gravel is easier than removing other types of planting mediums, so you might start with that and go through one season, while also experimenting with various plants.

a) **THE WICK SYSTEM:** This is a passive, non-recovery, system that uses no pump. With this system, the roots get nutrients through capillary action. Candle or oil-lamp wicking can be used for this. Nutrient-rich water from the fish tank (the reservoir) moves up the wicking and is held in the medium. Vermiculite, perlite, and sand can be used as a medium. This system is extremely easy to set up, and even easier to maintain, but it is not the most effective way to garden hydroponically.

b) THE EBB AND FLOW SYSTEM: This is an active, recovery-type system, whereby a submersible pump, placed in the reservoir (the fish tank), pumps the nutrient-rich water to the plant troughs where it's delivered to the roots of the plants. The BIODOME GARDEN uses a modified ebb-and-flow system. With a true ebb-and-flow system the solution is pumped into trays, where it remains for twenty to thirty minutes before being drained off, which is called a flood cycle. As the solution drains back into the reservoir, it pulls oxygen-poor air into the medium, allowing the roots ample oxygen for maximum nutrient intake. But with the BIODOME GARDEN, oxygen is continually delivered to the roots as the water moves past them.

(4) NUTRIENTS: Like soil, hydroponic systems need to be fertilized, and the three major nutrients for both soil and hydroponic systems are nitrogen, potassium, and phosphorous. Plants search out these nutrients naturally when growing in soil, but with hydroponics, the nutrients need to be present in the solution and delivered to the root zone. If any of the nutrients are missing, problems arise. Commercial hydroponic fertilizers are in a more refined form, and with fewer impurities, than organic fertilizers, making them more stable and soluble, while organic fertilizers depend on the action of microbes and bacteria to break down the nutritional elements for easier absorption by the plant roots.

(5) MICRONUTRIENTS: For healthy plant growth, in addition to nitrogen, potassium, and phosphorous, plants also need trace elements, called micronutrients. Micronutrients include sulfur, boron, iron, cobalt, calcium, iron, magnesium, copper, and molybdenum. If any of these are missing, plants become stressed and susceptible to pests, bacteria and fungus, and if they survive, they will produce poor yields. So it's essential that plants receive all of the nutrients they need in order to stay healthy and produce high yields of high-quality fruit or vegetables. With the aquaculture system incorporated in the BIODOME GARDEN, nutrient-rich water is delivered constantly to the plants in the hydroponic troughs, as well as to the plants rooted in soil.

(6) GROWING MEDIUMS: Instead of soil, plants grown hydroponically are rooted in an inert medium, with a balanced, pH adjusted, nutrient solution delivered to the roots. The growing medium alone supplies no nutrition, but is simply something to aerate and support the root system of the plant while the nutrient-rich water passes through.

There are a wide range of growing mediums to choose from, but only a few will be discussed here. Perlite, vermiculite, soilless mixes, sand, and pea gravel are commonly-used mediums that are stable and don't effect the pH of the solution. They are also inexpensive, and all but pea gravel work well with a wicking system. Commercial soilless mixes are also available. These retain water and have good wicking action for hydroponic gardening.

a) **OASIS CUBES**: These are mentioned here because they are good for starting plants from seeds then transferring them into either a hydroponic garden or into soil. These are pre-formed cubes with a neutral pH. They are available in several sizes, all of which retain water well. Once the plants are up, they can be transplanted directly into the growing medium without disturbing the roots.

b) **PERLITE**: This is a growing medium mined from volcanic glass. Perlite is one of the favorite hydroponic growing mediums. Because of the shape of the particles, air passages are formed, which provide optimum aeration. Perlite is also sterile, so it is free of insects, seeds and disease. It is often mixed half-and-half with vermiculite. Because it has an especially good wicking action, it is frequently used in wick-type systems. It is also fairly inexpensive. One warning though. It is not good to inhale the dust from perlite, so you should wear a dust mask when mixing perlite with other mediums, as well as when filling the hydroponic troughs.

c) **VERMICULITE**: Another mined material, vermiculite resembles mica in its natural state. It's often mixed with perlite because perlite doesn't retain water and nutrients well, yet is a good oxygenator, while vermiculite readily retains moisture, so these growing mediums balance each other. A 50/50 mix works well for both wicking and the adapted ebb-and-flow system used in the BIODOME GARDEN.

d) **SOILLESS MIXES**: Most soilless mixes contain spaghnam moss, vermiculite and perlite, so they retain water and have good wicking action. These mixes can contain fine particles that can clog pumps, so you'll need to contain the pump in some kind of filter, such as putting it in a nylon stocking and tying a knot in the end.

e) SAND: This medium is readily available, inexpensive, and holds water while allowing good aeration for oxygenating, so it is a good medium for wicking. But unlike perlite, it is not a health hazard to breathe.

e) PEA GRAVEL: This is also an inexpensive growing medium, but because the water drains right out, it cannot be used for wicking.

(7) MAINTAINING PROPER pH: In order for plants to use nutrients in a hydroponic system, the nutrients must be dissolved in the solution. pH refers to the hydrogen-hydroxylion content of a solution, and it is a measure of the acidity or alkalinity of that solution. When the pH is at the wrong level, plants lose their ability to absorb some of the nutrients required for healthy growth.

a) ACID OR ALKALINE: Solutions ionize into positive and negative ions. If the solution has more hydrogen (positive) ions than hydroxyl (negative) ions, it's an acid solution that ranges on the pH scale between 1.0 and 6.9. Conversely if the solution has more hydroxyl ions than hydrogen, it's an alkaline (or base) solution, with a range between 7.1 and 14 on the pH scale. 7 is neutral, and pure water is 7.

b) THE pH SCALE IS LOGARITHMIC: Because the pH scale is logarithmic, each unit of change represents a tenfold change in the hydrogen-hydroxylion concentration. This means that a 5.0 solution is ten times more acidic than a 6.0 solution.

c) KEEPING THE BALANCE: Because, in hydroponic gardening, plants get all of their nutrients from the solution, control of pH is very important. When the pH of a solution rises above 6.5 some of the nutrients and micro-nutrients begin to precipitate out of solution and can stick to the walls of the tank. As an example, iron, at a pH level of 7.3, will be about half precipitated, and at around 8.0 there is pretty much no iron left in solution. Conversely, some nutrients will precipitate out of solution when the pH drops. Once the nutrients have precipitated out of solution, plants are unable to absorb them and they begin to suffer deficiencies and eventually die if left uncorrected.

d) DIFFERENT PLANTS HAVE DIFFERENT pH REQUIREMENTS: In general, most plants prefer a slightly acid growing environment between 5.8 and 6.8, with 6.3 being optimum. Below is a list of pH ranges for some common plants, but information for other plants is available on the internet or other sources:

Plant	pH Range
Pumpkin	5.0-6.5
Strawberries	5.5-6.5
Tomatoes	5.5-6.5
Carrots	5.8-6.4
Cucumbers	5.8-6.0
Beans	6.0-6.5
Broccoli	6.0-6.5
Chives	6.0-6.5
Garlic	6.0-6.5
lettuce	6.0-6.5
peas	6.0-6.8
Radish	6.0-7.0
Cantaloupe	6.5-6.8
Onions	6.5-7.0
Cabbage	6.5-7.5

e) CHECKING THE pH: The pH in a hydroponic system is much easier to check than the pH of soil. pH-Testing kits can be purchased from pet stores that sell fish and aquarium supplies, hydroponic supply stores and even most hardware stores. The pH should be checked regularly and adjusted as needed by adding small amounts of potash to raise the pH, or small amounts of phosphoric acid to lower it. Following are several ways to check the pH in a hydroponic system.

1) PAPER TEST STRIPS: These are paper strips that are impregnated with pH-sensitive dye, which changes color when dipped into the solution. The color is then compared with a color chart to determine the pH. Whereas test strips are inexpensive and easy to use, they can be hard to read because the differences in color can be very subtle.

2) LIQUID pH TEST KITS: With these kits, pH is determined by adding a few drops of pH-sensitive dye to a small amount of the solution and comparing the color with a color chart. This is more accurate than the test-strip method and easier to read.

3) DIGITAL METERS: The most accurate and popular method of testing pH is the digital meter in the form of a digital pen. Measuring the pH amounts to dipping the electrode of the pen into the water and waiting a few seconds. The pH value will be displayed on an LCD screen. Whereas digital meters are very accurate when properly calibrated--which they need often--they take a lot of care or they'll stop working.

f) ORGANIC HYDROPONIC GARDENING: When organic fertilizers are used in the water, the system is said to be an Organic Hydroponic Garden. One of the benefits of organic hydroponics is that organic fertilizers are more forgiving than chemical fertilizers, which burn plants if used in excess. With organic fertilizers, nutrient-rich water is absorbed by the roots up to the saturation point, while the growing medium absorbs and retains nutrients as well.

g) SELF-ADJUSTING pH: There are three common problems associated with hydroponic gardening: 1) maintaining the level of nutrients in the water; 2) maintaining the supply of nutrients; 3) and maintaining the pH balance of water. The temperature of the water, the fertilizer used, the type of growing medium in use, the kind of plants being grown, and even the age of the plants, all effect the pH. However, because of the aquaculture in the fish tank, chemicals that are normally used to adjust the pH in hydroponic gardening (mostly phosphoric acid to lower it, and potassium hydroxide to raise it) can't be used. On the other hand, with an aquaculture system in place, pH tends to self-regulate because the aquatic animals present in the water guarantee a constant supply of nutrients, which satisfies problems 1 and 2 above. And because the fertilizer is organic, there is less concern with maintaining the pH balance, so most of the problems associated with hydroponic gardening are eliminated. But if pH does become an issue, a food grade citric acid can be used to lower the pH, and potassium bicarbonate can be used to raise it. These natural pH adjusters can be purchased in crystallized form from online suppliers

STAYING IN CONTROL

Companions: Plants and Bugs

Healthy plants are more resistant to disease than unhealthy plants, and when the ecological balance within a green house begins to break down, the biological life within also decreases, making plants weak, low in food production, and susceptible to disease and insect attack. So the first step in controlling insect infestation is to focus on the soil, because plants need humus and organic matter to survive. The humus holds moisture in the soil, making nutrients more available to the plants' roots, while also holding the particles together, thus preventing erosion. And the organic matter in the soil feeds all the organisms and releases nutrients. Chapter 5 discussed building up the soil, so at this point your vegetable beds should be filled with dark, crumbly, organic soil rich in nutrients and crawling with earthworms. So now you are ready to plant your crops.

DIVERSITY IS THE KEY: Another thing to consider is that, as with other insects, beneficial insects have different feeding requirements during the stages of their development. During some stages in their life cycles they eat pest insects, but during other stages they eat only nectar and pollen, so a diversity of plants is essential to attracting beneficial insects. By choosing companion plants and laying it out on paper before planting, you'll help your plants with natural insecticide repellants and attractants, which is as important as attracting beneficial insects.

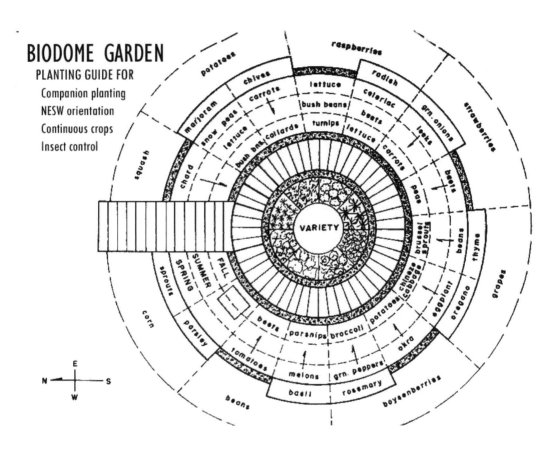

It's good to lay it all out on paper before planting

COMPANION PLANTS: When choosing companion plants you need to consider several factors. First, never plant heavy feeders next to each other. They'll compete for the nutrients and neither will flourish. However, if you put caraway plants throughout your garden, they'll help to loosen the soil. There are numerous books available on companion planting, and many websites with lists of plant "friends" so it won't be covered in depth here, but included will be a short list of some common herb and plant combinations to include in your BIODOME GARDEN to get your started.

81

VEGETABLE	VEGETABLE COMPANIONS
Asparagus	tomatoes, parsley, marigold, basil
Beets	lettuce, onions, cabbage, bush beans, broccoli, garlic, Chinese cabbage, kale, cauliflower, kohlrabi
Broccoli	Swiss chard, celery, onions, beets, dill, garlic, cucumbers, nasturtium, potatoes, rosemary, sage, spinach, mint, lettuce
Brussels Sprouts	Swiss chard, beets, spinach, celery, sage, cucumbers, rosemary, dill, potatoes, garlic, onions, hussop, nasturtium, mint, lettuce
Bush Beans	carrots, corn, Swiss chard, peas, cabbage, strawberries, Chinese cabbage, kohlrabi, Brussels sprouts, radishes, garlic, celery, broccoli, potatoes, eggplants, cauliflower, beets, cucumbers
Cabbage	beets, Swiss chard, celery, spinach, cucumbers, dill, potatoes, lettuce, mint, cucumbers, nasturtium, sage, rosemary, onions
Carrots	beans, tomatoes, chives, sage, lettuce, rosemary, onions, radishes, peas, peppers
Cauliflower	celery, lettuce, Swiss chard, beets, potatoes, onions, mint, nasturtium, beans, garlic, rosemary, spinach, sage, cucumbers
Celery	broccoli, tomatoes, dill, Brussels sprouts, nasturtium, cauliflower, Chinese cabbage, garlic, kale, chives, kohlrabi
Corn	beans, melons, cucumbers, parsley, pumpkin, potatoes, squash. peas
Cucumber	beans, Brussels sprouts, broccoli, cabbage, Chinese cabbage, cauliflower, corn, kohlrabi, kale, nasturtium, marigold, oregano, peas, radishes, tomatoes
Eggplant	beans, peppers, marigold
Kale	beets, cucumbers, celery, garlic, dill, hyssop, mint, lettuce, nasturtium, potatoes, onions, sage, rosemary, spinach, chard
Kohlrabi	beets, cucumbers, dill, celery, hyssop, garlic, potatoes, nasturtium, lettuce, mint, onions, Swiss chard, rosemary, sage, spinach
Lettuce	broccoli, beets, onions, cabbage, cauliflower, chives, Brussels sprouts, kale, garlic, strawberries, radishes, kohlrabi, carrots
Melons	marigold, corn, oregano, pumpkin, nasturtium, radish, squash
Onions	broccoli, beets, cabbage, Brussels sprouts, chamomile, carrots, Chinese cabbage, cauliflower, kale, kohlrabi, peppers, strawberries, lettuce, summer savory, Swiss chard, tomatoes
Parsley	asparagus, corn, tomatoes
Peas	carrots, chives, cucumbers, mint, beans, corn, radish, turnip
Peppers	carrots, eggplants, tomato onions

Pole beans	Brussels sprouts, broccoli, cabbage, carrots, kale, eggplant, cauliflower, Chinese cabbage, corn, cucumbers, garlic, celery, kohlrabi, peas, potatoes, radishes, strawberries, Swiss chard
Potatoes	kale, broccoli, cabbage Brussels sprouts, Chinese cabbage, corn eggplant, horseradish, kohlrabi, beans, marigold, peas
Pumpkins	corn, melons, marigolds, nasturtium, oregano, squash
Radishes	beans, carrots, cucumbers, chervil, melons, lettuce, peas, nasturtium
Spinach	broccoli, Brussels sprouts, cauliflower, kale, kohlrabi, Chinese cabbage, strawberries
Strawberry	borage, beans, onions, lettuce, spinach, thyme
Summer squash	corn, marigold, borage, nasturtium, oregano, pumpkins
Swiss chard	broccoli, kale, cabbage, Brussels sprouts, Chinese cabbage, cabbage, beans, kohlrabi, onions
Tomatoes	asparagus, bee balm, borage, basil, carrots, chives, celery, cucumbers, mint, onions, peppers, parsley, marigold
Turnips	peas
Winter Squash	melons, corn, pumpkins, nasturtium, oregano, borage

THE IMPORTANCE OF INCLUDING HERBS: Planting borage with squash, tomatoes and strawberries helps keep tomato worms from attacking. Dead nettle and horseradish planted with potatoes keep potato bugs away. Rosemary is a good companion to cabbage, beans, carrots, and sage, as it works to keep the cabbage moths away. However, some plants should be kept away from other plants at all costs. Dill should never be planted with carrots or caraway. Keep cucumbers at opposite sides of the garden from sage. And Fennel should not be included at all.

A FEW HERBS TO INCLUDE:

- Mint and rosemary discourage many egg-laying insects, including the cabbage moth
- Basil shoos off flies and mosquitoes
- Borage will fend off tomato worms
- Marigolds ward off Japanese beetles
- Thyme repels cabbage worms
- Spinach deters slugs.
- Chives and leeks deter the carrot fly
- Garlic repels almost all bugs, including aphids and Japanese beetles
- Lavender and dill grow well with cilantro

A SPECIAL WORD ABOUT CILANTRO: This pungent herb, sometimes known as Mexican parsley, draws beneficial insects that are attracted to its tiny flowers. Parasitoid wasps and hoverflies are just two of the beneficial insects attracted to cilantro, which can be tucked between tomato plants, and planted among rows of spinach and other vegetables throughout the planting bed. However, cilantro is short-lived, so it will need to be reseeded every few weeks. You might want to select a variety that bolts easily and produces flowers quickly. Basil, mint and yarrow are good companions to cilantro, but fennel should not be planted nearby.

COMPANION PLANTING AND FLAVOR: Did you know that if you plant sweet basil next to tomatoes, beans and squash, the vegetables will taste better? Thyme, sage, and bee balm are also good flavor companions with tomatoes. And lovage, marjoram, and tarragon enhance the flavor of almost any vegetable they are paired with. However, strong herbs can actually change the scents and flavors of other herbs and vegetables. If spearmint is planted next to peppermint, in time they'll both taste the same. So flavor also needs to be considered when planting.

Rosemary helps keep cabbage moths away

ATTRACTING GOOD BUGS AND REPELLING BAD ONES

While a number of plants can be added to the garden to repel harmful insects, certain pungent herbs should be included to attract beneficial ones (AKA beneficials), so one of the most compelling reasons for companion planting is the ability of certain plants to attract beneficials that feed on destructive insects like caterpillars and aphids. Beneficials are also the reason why insecticides, even natural ones, should not be used at random.

HOW BENEFICIALS WORK: Beneficial insects use various means of destroying harmful pests, including laying eggs on plant leaves. After hatching, the larvae feed on pests that are attacking the leaves, eliminating the next life cycle of that pest. Insects also have different feeding requirements during various stages of their development. During some stages in the life cycle, beneficial insects feast on pest insects, but during other stages, their diets are confined to nectar and pollen, so a diversity of plant material is essential to attracting and maintaining them. But also keep in mind that both good and bad insects are scavengers that are attracted to rotting plant material, so it's important to always clean up the rotten fruit or vegetables, as well as any diseased leaves and plants.

WHAT'S NEEDED TO ATTRACT BENEFICIALS:
- Shady, protected areas for beneficials to lay eggs
- Low growing plants as cover for ground beetles, such as thyme, rosemary, mint, coriander, dill, clovers, yarrow, and rue
- Tiny flowers for miniscule predatory wasps
- Composite flowers (daisy and chamomile) and mints (spearmint, peppermint, or catnip) to attract predatory wasps, hover flies, and robber flies

BENEFICIALS THAT ARE WELCOME: There is a long list to include, but for the purpose of this book, only a few will be discussed.
- Ladybugs feed on aphids
- Lacewing larvae feed on aphids
- Ground beetles feed on ground-dwelling pests.
- Parasitoid wasps feed on aphids, caterpillars and grubs
- Hover flies feed on many insects including leafhoppers and caterpillars
- Preying mantis eat everything!

PARASITOIDS & PREDATOR INSECTS AS BIOLOGICAL CONTROLS:

BENEFICIAL INSECTS	WHAT THEY CONTROL (SAMPLING)
Nematodes	grubs, beetles, cutworms, army worms
Ladybugs	aphids, Colorado potato beetle
Green lacewings	aphids, mealy bugs, thrips, spider mites
Praying Mantis	almost any insect
Trichogramma wasp	corn borer, cabbage looper, other worms
Pirate Bug	thrips, mites, aphids, caterpillars, bollworms

BIOLOGICAL CONTROLS: Aphids, slugs, white flies, caterpillars and other garden pests thrive in the greenhouse environment, but insect pests and plant diseases don't just happen. They're usually caused by plant stress from light, water, temperature, or nutrient imbalance. Overwatering can lead to high humidity, which encourages plant disease, so keeping the air inside the BIODOME GARDEN moving is crucial. As for bugs... nature's means of regulating the population of insects is by relying on parasites and predators to keep organisms under control. But before any biological control practice can begin, it's necessary to identify the problem.

(1) IDENTIFYING THE PROBLEM: Sometimes what's perceived to be an insect problem is actually a plant disease. Plant diseases can be caused by fungi, bacteria, viruses and other organisms. Lack of certain nutrients can also mimic diseases or insect attack. It's also important to recognize the different stages of insect development. Small larvae with six spots on their backs will likely become ladybugs, which are beneficial. Also, different stages of development are more damaging than others. It's also not necessary to kill every harmful bug in the garden. Large plants close to harvest can tolerate more damage than tiny seedlings.

a) CHEWING INSECTS: This insect group is easy to classify: plant leaves have been chewed. Many chewing insects are easy to spot, such as the Japanese beetle, or the Colorado potato beetle, or the numerous species of caterpillars such as tomato hornworm or tent caterpillar. But some chewing insects only come out at night, then burrow back into the soil during the day, so all that's left for detection are the chomped leaves. This can be the case if young plants disappear over night, and only the stub of a stem is left behind.

Caterpillars chew holes in leaves, stems, flowers and fruit

b) **SUCKING INSECTS**: These insects are very damaging to plants and also carry diseases that are spread from plant to plant. Sucking insects do damage by inserting their mouth parts into the plant tissues and sucking out the juices. If the leaves on certain plants become puckered, curled or misshapen, you should suspect sucking insects. These insects tend to collect underneath the leaves, so start by looking there. Common sucking insects include mites, mealy bugs, aphids, leafhoppers and thrips.

c) **BORING INSECTS**: These insects bore into plant stems, leaves, and fruit, disrupting the plant's ability to transport water. This also creates the perfect opportunity for disease organisms to enter the plant through the holes. If you find small accumulations of sawdust-like material on the stems, leaves, or fruit, you can suspect boring insects. Examples of these include corn and squash vine borers.

d) **DISEASED ORGANISMS**: There are several ways that disease organisms can attack plants. Some produce toxins that replace plant tissue with their own, or kill the plant outright, some attack leaf surfaces, limiting the plant's ability to carry on photosynthesis, and some produce substances that clog plant tissues that transport water and nutrients. The presence of mushroom-like growths with grayish mildew appearance on leaves are a sign of a plant disease. Spots on leaves are another. Some disease organisms live in the soil for years, others are brought in by insects or with infected plant material. Planting resistant varieties, rotating crops, and removing diseased plants or the diseased areas of plants (but NOT to the compost bin) will limit the spread of diseases.

e) NUTRITIONAL DEFICIENCIES: This is evident when you see stunted growth or the yellowing or reddening of leaves. Excessive vegetative growth and little fruiting, which makes plants more susceptive to disease and insect problems, can indicate too much nitrogen. Plants that have adequate nutrients are better able to resist attacks from both diseases and insects. Nutrition also includes water. High humidity can encourage some disease species, but proper watering through irrigation to the soil instead of to the leaves, and good aeration of plants by adequate spacing will help offset this.

BAD BUGS AND GOOD BUGS

BAD VEGETABLE GARDEN PESTS: If you want to stay organic, never resort to chemical insecticides, but instead, use predators and parasites to control the plant pests that are inevitable in a greenhouse environment. The most common vegetable garden pests include aphids, beetles, caterpillars, mealy bugs, thrips, scales, and white flies. Following is a brief rundown of each:

(1) BEETLES: There are many kinds of beetles, usually less than a half inch in size. They can be spotted, striped, or in solid, often iridescent colors. They attack plants by chewing holes in their leaves, stems, flowers and fruit. Included in this category are potato beetles, cucumber beetles, bean beetles and flea beetles, just to name a few. Beneficial insects that can be introduced to control beetles include lady bugs, preying mantis, and beneficial nematodes.

Lady bugs go after beetles, that chew holes in leaves, stems and flowers

(2) CATERPILLARS: Like beetles, caterpillars destroy plants by chewing holes in their leaves, stems, flowers and fruit. Caterpillars can be striped along the back or side, green, brown, cream, and in a variety of colors and patterns. In length, they can be less than an inch long to several inches long. Garden pests include tomato pinworms, cutworms and hornworms. Beneficial insects used to control caterpillars include green lacewings, pirate bugs, preying mantis and trichogramma wasps.

Caterpillars and beetles are chewing insects that leave holes in plants

(3) MEALY BUGS: These bugs suck the juices out of plants, causing the leaves to wilt and drop off, weakening plants, that quickly decline from damage. Mealy bugs are soft-bodied and are covered with a waxy powder. Beneficial bugs that can be introduced to control mealy bugs include lady bugs and green lace wings. Daubing mealy bugs with alcohol or washing them off with soap works well.

(4) WHITEFLIES: These insects suck out the juices of plants, weakening them and leaving them susceptible to disease. Adult whiteflies resemble tiny moths, are light-colored, and swarm in a cloud when an infested plant is disturbed. Young whiteflies are usually found on the underside of leaves, and they are pale green in color.

(5) APHIDS: Aphids are the most common vegetable garden insect pests. Ants keep them in their nests during the winter and place them on host plants in the spring. The aphids produce honeydew, which the ants eat, so controlling the ants often solves the aphid problem. Aphid feed in colonies, which is part of the reason why they are so destructive. Colonies of aphids can me found on new shoots, the underside of leaves, on twigs, and on branches, causing the plant leaves to curl and dry out. As they feed, they leave a residue on the plants called *aphid honey dew*, and if the infestation is large, a brownish-black fungi will start to grow on the leaves. This fungi, or *sooty mold*, covers the leaves, and the only way to get rid of the fungus is to get rid of the aphids. But it's the aphid honey dew that adult green lacewing feed on. But whereas the adult lacewing eats honeydew, the larvae of the lacewing eats the aphids. In addition to lacewings, ladybugs and praying mantis also prey on aphids. Aphids can also be sprayed with a mild soapy solution by mixing 1 tablespoon of Castile soap into 1 gallon of water. The soap strips them of their protective wax coating, thereby dehydrating them. Other means of repelling aphids are to squash several aphids around infested plants, which releases a chemical signal for the aphids to drop from the plant and leave. A garlic oil spray can also kill aphids and other soft-bodied insects, as will a dusting of diatomaceous earth. Repellant plants include anise, garlic, chives, petunias, radish and cilantro.

Aphids live and feed in colonies

90

(6) SCALE INSECTS: These tiny insects are often less than a 1/4 inch long, so a hand lens may be needed to see then. But their presence is known from the damage they cause to plants by sucking the juices out of leaves, causing them to yellow, turn silvery, curl and die. Yellow dots can also develop. When scale insects are present, plants quickly deteriorate and die. When an infestation of scales is heavy, the scales form filmy webs. Scales come in almost any color and are often eight-legged, such as spider mites, which can be found on the underside of leaves. Bugs used to control scale insects are lady bugs, green lace wings and praying mantis. Oil sprays are also effective.

(7) THRIPS: These small, yellow or black insects, which measure in at only 1/25 of an inch, scrape leaves and flowers and suck out the juices, leaving plant portions to curl and turn brown. Thrips go after tomatoes, beans, corn, and squash. Because they are so small, thrips are hard to detect, but if the plants show damage you can shake the plant over a piece of white paper and it will be dotted with small brown fecal pellets. Both the adults and the nymphs feed on plants. Predator bugs include beneficial nematodes, green lacewings, pirate bugs and ladybugs. Garlic and onion sprays are a good repellant.

(8) TOMATO HORNWORMS: These huge bugs destroy tomatoes, dill, eggplant, potato, and peppers. They are hard to find, and they leave a trail of defoliated stems. Look for greenish-yellow eggs laid singly on the undersides of leaves. Insect predators include lacewings, lady bugs and trichogramma wasps. Hornworms can also be controlled by directly spraying them with tea made from petunia leaves or insecticidal soap. Basil and marigolds work as repellants, and some gardeners claim that if you sprinkle cornmeal around plants infested with hornworms, the hornworms will eat the cornmeal and die because they can't digest it. Hornworms with white pouches on their backs indicate the presence of parasitic wasps, which are growing inside the pouches and will later hatch out. The wasp larva in turn kill the hornworms.

(9) MITES: Mites are tiny members of the arachnid family that can produce up to sixteen generations per season. There are many species in colors of black, brown, green, red or yellow. Mites suck the chlorophyll out of plant tissue, leaving dried out leaves with yellow or red spots, and blotches sometimes with tiny white dots. This is followed by a fine dusty looking webbing between leaves. If you tap the leaves over white paper, the mites will drop off. Predators of mites include ladybugs and green lacewings, and repellant plants include dill and coriander. In fact, a mix of 1/2 ounce coriander oil in 24 ounces of water will kill them when used as a spray. Mites can also be suffocated by mixing one cup of buttermilk and two cups of wheat flour into five gallons or water and spraying it onto them. It doesn't hurt the plants, and after a few hours, it can be washed off.

GOOD VEGETABLE GARDEN INSECTS: A healthy organic garden relies on a delicate balance of prey and predator species of insects to maintain control of the bad bugs, in addition to cutting away and destroying portions of plants that are diseased or suffer from heavy infestations of pests. Larger bugs such as beetles can be hand picked, and caterpillars can be rubbed from stems and foliage, and the bugs dropped into a container of alcohol. There are numerous parasitoids and predator insects available for purchase from suppliers, but to get you started, only praying mantids, green lacewings, ladybugs, beneficial nematodes, trichogramma wasps, and pirate bugs will be discussed because these six are vital to keeping plant damaging insects under control.

(1) BENEFICIAL NEMATODES: Not to be confused with destructive nematodes, beneficial nematodes are small microscopic worms that live below the soil. They are the best predators of over 250 pests that spend any stage of their life cycle in the soil, killing most before they become adults, while leaving plants and earthworms alone. A single nematode enters an insect through its skin or natural openings and releases a toxic bacteria that kills the insect, usually within a day or two. Beneficial nematodes are easy to introduce into the soil. Simply mix the contents of the packet purchased in a bucket of water and drench the soil. One million treats approximately 2000 square feet. Beneficial nematodes destroy ants, army worms, beetles, bark beetle, cucumber beetle, June beetles, Japanese beetles, leaf beetles, Pine beetles, flea beetles, black fly larvae, Billbugs, cabbage worms, cinch bugs, coddling moths, Colorado potato beetle, cranberry girdler, cutworm, fleas, flies, fungus gnats, gall gnats, grubs, loopers, mole cricket, Mormon cricket, saw flies, sod webworms, soil-dwelling pests, squash bugs, termites, boll weevil, root weevil, vine weevil, white grubs.

(2) LADYBUGS (OR BEETLES): Both adults & larvae feed on aphids, each ladybug consuming as many as 5,000 aphids during their one-year lifetime. They also scavenge mites, eggs, and a wide variety soft-bodied insects that include bollworms, Colorado potato beetle, leafhoppers, leafworms, mealy bugs, scale insects and thrips. Like many brightly-colored insects, ladybugs are distasteful to predators, secreting an odorous, unpleasant fluid out of their joints when disturbed. Apart from aphids, ladybugs need a source of pollen for food, and are attracted to specific types of plants, especially those with umbrella-shaped flowers such as cilantro, dill, and caraway. Other plants that attract ladybugs are geraniums and dandelions, which can be planted among the vegetables. Ladybugs do not reproduce in the greenhouse environment so they will need to be reintroduced as needed.

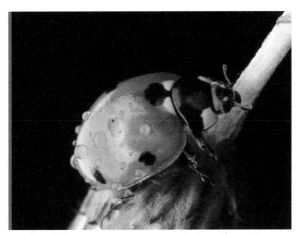

Ladybugs prey on a variety of pests

(3) GREEN LACEWING LARVAE: Commonly called the *Aphid Lion*, the lacewing larvae is a voracious predator, feeding on many different species of insects with soft bodies, mites & eggs, but their primary food is aphids. During a two to four week period, a lacewing can consume up to 600 aphids, using mandibles with which to pierce prey and suck out their body juices. Adult lacewing eat pollen, nectar, and honeydew, the sugary liquid discharged by aphids. Because lacewings thrive in humid environments, they are ideal in a greenhouse. They are effective in controlling pests on potatoes, tomatoes, peppers, eggplants, strawberries, and sweet corn. In addition to aphids, lacewing also prey on scale bugs, bollworms, cutworms, fruit worms, leafworms, caterpillars, mealy bugs, spider mites, whiteflies, thrips, eggs of leafhoppers, moths, and beetle larvae.

Green Lacewing

(4) PRAYING MANTIS: Depending on gender, the praying mantis is 3-4 inches long and is closely related to the grasshopper, cockroach and other stick insects. With a voracious appetite, the praying mantis will feed on just about any insect pest, having been known to consume up to 16 crickets a day. It starts life in an egg, and when the nymph hatches, it's first meal is apt to be a sibling mantis, of which it can have several hundred--the amount of young mantids from each egg case. It initially eats eggs, aphids, mites, mosquitoes and leafhoppers, but as it grows, it moves on to spiders, moths, grasshoppers, and beetles, as well as caterpillars, larvae, and other soft-bodied insects. The mantis is the only known insect that can turn its head and look over its shoulder, which allows it to lie in wait for any unsuspecting pray and snap it up with the lightening movement of its forelegs. These large, solitary, slow moving insects are the only insects that feed at night on moths, and the only predator insect quick enough to catch mosquitoes and flies.

Praying mantis eat just about anything!

94

(5) PIRATE BUGS: Tiny oval-shaped pirate bugs range from 1/12 to 1/5 inch long when adult, are black to irridescent purple with white markings and triangular heads. Nymphs are yellowish to reddish brown, pear-shaped, and have red eyes. Eggs are inserted into plant tissues, so they are difficult to detect. Both adults and nymphs feed on insect eggs as well as small insects such as thrips, mites, aphids, whiteflies, small caterpillars, bollworms, army worms, coddling moths, cutworms, fruit worms, leafworms, spider mites and psyllids, killing them by piercing them with their mouth parts and sucking out their body fluids. Pirate bugs are common insect predators in many crops, including corn, small grains, soybeans and tomatoes. If prey is abundant, they will kill more than they need to survive.

(6) TRICHOGRAMMA WASPS: Being the size of some bacteria, these wasps are one of the smallest insects on the planet. They lay their eggs inside the eggs of over two hundred species of moths, preventing them from hatching into caterpillars that feed on plants. Although they are microscopic, they still look like wasps, with constricted abdomens, short antennae, red eyes, two pair of wings and an ovipositor, or stinger, on the female. When you purchase them from a supplier they come shipped while parasitized in the host egg, and you receive what looks like a piece of sandpaper, but this piece of paper has been inoculated with approximately 5000 eggs. 24,000 trichogramma will treat up to 1000 square feet. Trichogramma go after cabbageworm, cutworms, bollworms, caterpillars, coddling moths, leafworms, cane borers, earworms, tomato hornworms, corn Earworms, web worms, cabbage loopers, fruitworms, corn Borers, and army worms.

One of several species of predatory wasps

95

(7) DECOLLATE SNAIL: The decollate snail is added here because it is an effective predator against slugs and brown garden snails, moving slowly about the BIODOME GARDEN while looking for egg masses of slugs and snails, while also attacking the smaller brown garden snail. They do not eat healthy plants, but do eat old leaf mulch. They are night feeders, living in the top few inches of soil during the day and coming out to hunt once the sun goes down. Decollate snails live for two years, laying around two hundred eggs a year. Once introduced into the garden and working, slugs and brown garden snails will begin to disappear.

OTHER MEANS OF RESOLVING THE PROBLEM

(1) HANDPICKING: Some insect control can be as easy as removing the bugs by hand and dropping them into soapy water. But use caution when handling bugs. Some bite, some sting, and some excrete oily substances that can cause injury to humans, so when handling unfamiliar insects, it's best to wear gloves or pick them off with tweezers.

(2) SPRAYING WITH WATER: Another method of removing insects is by spraying them off the plants with a hose. One problem with this method, along with having to gather up the bugs for disposal, is that spraying plants can lead to fungi and other diseases on the leaves, especially in hot, humid weather. It also subjects the plants to damage from the force of the water needed to wash off the bugs.

(3) INSECT TRAPS: This method can be effective for some insects. The variety of bug determines the style of trap needed, and because they are extremely species-specific, traps do not harm beneficial insects. These traps, in many cases, depend on the use of pheromones, which are the naturally-occurring chemicals produced by the bugs, to attract bugs of the opposite sex during mating. Other traps depend on color and a sticky surface to lure and catch bugs. However, traps can also draw bugs to the area, so they should not be placed inside the BIODOME GARDEN, but nearby, where they will draw insects *out* of the planting bed.

(4) ORGANIC PESTICIDES: Numerous combinations of household products can be as effective as chemical pesticides in controlling bugs in the BIODOME GARDEN. This can be as simple as mixing hot sauce in water or just using an organic soap and water mix to spray directly onto the plants. Soap mixed with any concoction has the added benefit of reducing the chance of diseased plants. It's also extremely effective in controlling many soft-bodied insects such as aphids and whiteflies. Be sure to use only non-toxic, biodegradable liquid soaps and dishwashing detergents though. The recipes listed below should help discourage or eliminate such organisms as aphids, cutworms, thrips, tomato hornworm, slugs, beetles, moths, flies, ants, mites, spiders, and many other common garden pests.

(5) REPELLANTS: Because bugs are attracted to plants because of their fragrance, it makes sense that foul-smelling substances such as tobacco, garlic, and pungent herbs like basil, rosemary, chives, basil, oregano and sage will repel them. Proportions of ingredients can vary widely but all can be effective.

ORGANIC PESTICIDES, REPELLANTS & ATTRACTANTS

Organic and non-toxic pest control often get lumped into the same category. While non-toxic is much better than the toxic variety, many of the ingredients used to make non-toxic pest sprays contain non-organic brands of soap. These products, while not as dangerous as herbicides and pesticides, still contain toxic chemicals. So, if you're trying to be as earth friendly as possible, use only organic soaps or dishwashing detergents when preparing pesticides, otherwise any of the following recipes that include soap should be considered non-toxic rather than organic. Also, when applying sprays it's best to spray in the evening when the sun's not hot.

NATURAL AND ORGANIC PESTICIDES

ALL PURPOSE INSECTICIDE SPRAY: Alcohol sprays are effective on aphids, thrips, whiteflies, mealy bugs and scale insects.
>   1/2 cup rubbing alcohol
>   1 quart liquid soap

Mix directly into a spray container. Do not spray in direct sunlight as leaf damage may occur. Spray, then let sit for 20 minutes. Spray plant down with clear water to reduce foliage damage. Spray every 3 days for 2 weeks.

INSECTICIDAL VEGETABLE OIL: Vegetable oils suffocate the insect. For this pesticide, mix the following in large quantities and use it throughout the year:

> 1 Tbsp. dishwashing detergent
>
> 1 C. vegetable oil

Add 1 tablespoon of the solution to 1 cup of water and spray onto the insects and plants until the solution runs off. This is effective in controlling mites, aphids and a few other insects. Spray the solution in the evenings, but if the weather is hot, rinse off the plants in the morning so the oil doesn't burn the leaves.

GARLIC AND SOAP INSECTICIDE: This mixture helps rid the garden of sucking and chewing insects, leaf spot, mildew, and spore disease. It can also be sprayed directly on infested vegetables and flowers.

> 2 whole cayenne peppers
>
> 1 large onion
>
> 1 garlic bulb
>
> 1/4 cup water
>
> soap flakes

Whirl the peppers, onion, garlic and 1/4 cup of water in a blender or a food processor then transfer it to a large container. Add 1 gallon of water and 1 tablespoon of soap flakes and stir the mixture to blend. Allow it to stand for 24 hours, then strain it and use in a sprayer. The leftover mash can be buried among the plants where the infestations occur.

HOT-PEPPER SPRAY: Strain the following and spray, but hot peppers will burn the skin and eyes so take proper precautions.

> 1/2 cup of hot peppers chopped
>
> 2 cups of hot water

Peppers act as a repellant on some insects, but on softer insects an acidic burning effect takes place and kills them, especially if mixed with garlic.

BUTTERMILK SPRAY: This pesticide is effective against spider mites.

> 1/2 cup buttermilk
>
> 4 cups flour
>
> 1/2 gallon of water

Mix the flour, buttermilk and water together . Spray several applications over a two-day period to make sure the infestation has been eradicated.

SLUG BREW: This is a simple way to ridding your garden of slugs and it only has one ingredient: *Beer*. Place a shallow container with beer, buried partway in the ground so about 1/3 is above the dirt. Change the container as it begins to fill with slugs. Slugs are attracted to the fermented yeast in the beer and drown in it.

ONION AND CHILI SPRAY: This pesticide is effective against any leaf-eating insects, but has a limited effect against most scale and hard-surfaced pests.

>   4 hot chilies, chopped
>   4 large onions, chopped
>   2 bulbs garlic, chopped
>   1 pint hot soapy water

Mix all the ingredients with the soapy water and allow it to sit for 24 hours. Strain and add water enough water to use in a sprayer. It can be stored in a sealed container in a dark place for up to 2 weeks.

PYRETHRUM DAISY: The dried, powdered flowers of the pyrethrum daisy are an effective organic insecticide ingredient. Insects merely touching the substance are affected. The product works on flies, gnats, mosquitoes, spider mites, leafhoppers, stink bugs and aphids. Mix the dried powder with water and a few drops of liquid soap and spray it on fruits and vegetables

BAKING SODA: When mixed with water, baking soda has been shown to be effective in controlling some fungal diseases.

DIATOMACEOUS EARTH: This powder-like dust, which is made up of tiny marine organisms called diatoms, can be spread on the surface of the soil to reduce damage from soft-bodied insects and slugs. It is sharp and cuts or irritates soft organisms, causing them to dehydrate, yet is harmless to other organisms. Spread it on the soil before planting. It is effective against many soft-bodied insects, including cutworms, thrips, and slugs.

NATURAL AND ORGANIC REPELLANTS

SOFT SOAP SPRAY: This is best sprayed when the sun is low

>   6 tbsp Ivory Snow or flakes
>   1 gallon of water

CITRUS OIL: Commercial organic pesticides use steam-distilled orange peel to kill ants, cockroaches, weevils, locusts and fleas. A similar mixture can be prepared at home by boiling orange peels in water and left to steep overnight. Mix this with a vegetable oil and spray it directly on the plants. Add some baking soda and a tablespoon of liquid hot pepper sauce such as Tabasco, and bugs will leave.

BUG JUICE: You might want to use non-food utensils and wear plastic gloves for this. Start by collecting 1/2 cup of specific bug pests...

　　　1/4 cup of mashed bugs
　　　2 cups of water

Mix the bug juice with the water and add a few drops of soap, and spray.

GARLIC: Organic gardeners have known for decades that bugs are repelled by garlic. Planting garlic between rows of vegetables will help repel aphids, squash bugs, cabbage loppers, June bugs, and other insects, but spraying a garlic solution directly on the plants will assure it. Since bugs don't like hot and spicy, garlic can be combined with peppers, onions, vegetable oils and dishwashing soap. A quick and easy garlic spray is to mix equal parts of garlic, vinegar, onion, horseradish, and hot pepper and stir it into hot water. Let the mix sit overnight, then strain it and spray it directly on the plants.

GARLIC OIL SPRAY: This gets rid of aphids, cutworms, whiteflies, wireworms, slugs, and man other vegetable garden pests.

　　　1 medium onion, minced
　　　10-15 garlic cloves, crushed
　　　1 tablespoon cayenne pepper
　　　1 quart hot water
　　　1 tablespoon liquid dish soap

Soak the garlic, onion, and cayenne pepper in a pint of mineral oil for 24 hours. Add the water and mix. Strain it through a strainer and add the soap and apply it with a sprayer.

NASTURTIUM SPRAY: This spray is effective against aphids.

　　　1 cup nasturtium leaves
　　　1 cup of water.

Simmer the leaves in the water for 15 minutes, then cool and strain. Dilute the mixture with equal parts water, and apply with a sprayer.

HOMEMADE TOMATO LEAF SPRAY: This spray is effective against asparagus beetles and flea beetles, ear-worms and maggots.

    2 cups of chopped tomato leaves

    2 pints of water

    1/4 tsp of liquid soap

Soak the tomato leaves in water overnight, then strain out the tomato leaves and add another pint of water, along with the liquid soap. Spray foliage and soil as needed.

MOLASSES SPRAY: This is effective in controlling grasshoppers and caterpillars.

    3 tablespoons of molasses

    4 cups of warm water

Mix the molasses and water and apply using a spray bottle. Shake vigorously and spray the "Molasses Tea" directly on the plants every couple of days until the grasshoppers and caterpillars have left.

HOT PEPPER SPRAY: With this spray, the hotter the peppers, the more capsaicin, the more capsaicin, the better it will work to keep aphids away.

    1/2 cup of hot peppers such as jalapeno or cayenne

    2 cups of hot water

Chop the peppers and mix them into the hot water and let it sit overnight, then apply it to plants with a spray bottle. This works on other garden pests as well because most don't like the smell or the taste of hot peppers.

NATURAL AND ORGANIC ATTRACTANTS

GOOD BUG CHOW CONCENTRATE: This mix attracts ladybugs, green lacewings, parasitic wasps and other beneficial insects. Combine the following ingredients:

    2/3 cup of warm water

    4 tablespoons of brewer's yeast

    2 teaspoons of honey

    1/2 cup of sugar

Dilute 2 tablespoons of the concentrate in 1 quart of lukewarm water. Spray on plants in the spring and early summer. Don't spray plants when temperatures are over 80F. Store the mixture in a sealed container in the refrigerator so it won't go rancid. It will keep 7-10 days. The sugar is good for the plants.

SUGAR-WATER SPRAY: This attracts ladybugs. Mix the following thoroughly:

     32 ounces of warm water

     5 ounces of white sugar

Apply to the plants when aphids and other soft bodied insects are present and ladybugs will be attracted to the sugar water and go after the aphids.

Certain herbs make effective repellants and attractants

9 EASY-TO-BUILD ACCESSORIES

UTILIZING ALL THE SPACE UNDER THE DOME

The fiberglass dome on the cover of the book is fastened together with long connecting bolts that protrude inside the dome almost 2", offering an ideal place for hanging baskets or planters. The wires holding each planter are secured by a second nut that sandwiches the wire hangar between two nuts with two large washers. If your BIODOME GARDEN is covered by a fiberglass geodesic dome, hook eyes can be screwed into the wooden framework of the dome for holding hanging planters. Eight to ten planters can hang inside the dome this way. It's warmer up under the dome, and baskets tend to dry more quickly, so that has to be taken into account.

(1) HANGING PLANTERS OR BASKETS: The cedar hanging baskets in the photo above were purchased at a garden center, but an easy-to-build project at home would be to make hanging trays by cutting a 1"x12" cedar board into 12"x12" squares, which would be the bottoms of the trays, and enclosing them using 1"x6" cedar boards cut into 12" sections as side walls. Holes drilled in the top, center of each board are used for attaching the two wires that cross over from each side of the planters for hanging them from the connecting bolts or hook eyes inside the dome. Be sure to drill a 1" center hole in the bottom of each tray for drainage. Cover the hole with fiberglass screening, then add an inch of pea gravel to the bottom of each planter before filling them with potting soil. Cucumbers are growing in the planter in the photo above, but these 12"x12" planters are ideal for herbs, ensuring a continuous crop of fresh herbs well into the cold winter months, when they can he cut and either frozen or dried and used that way until a new crop can be planted. Some of the aromatic herbs also discourage bugs.

(2) INCLUDING MUSHROOM TRAYS: One of the advantages to raising mushrooms is that they can grow in parts of the BIODOME GARDEN that are useless for other purposes, such as under the utility sink, where nothing else will grow. Raising mushrooms from spores is relatively easy, and they can grow to maturity in less than two months. The key is to prepare a proper growing medium and to keep the spore moist and in a dark, cool area, away from sharp temperature fluctuations. Because mushrooms like darkness, trays can be stacked. The area under the sink provides room for trays 24"x30" and 6" deep. These trays can be made from 1"x12" cedar boards for the bottoms, cut to 30" lengths (two of these boards make up the bottoms of the trays), and 1"x6" cedar boards cut to fit the sides. Next, the bedding or substrate for growing mushrooms must be prepared.

a) PREPARE THE SUBSTRATE: The medium that mushrooms grow in is called substrate. This can be made of fresh, damp manure with straw, and even coffee grinds. Sawdust from untreated hardwood can also be added. Shiitake mushrooms grow well in hardwood sawdust, while oyster mushrooms like straw, and white buttons thrive in composted manure, so you can adjust your mixture to whichever variety of mushroom you intend to grow. Try one variety and see how it does, then experiment with another after that crop is done. The manure, straw, sawdust substrate can be mixed in a bin made from 2X12 untreated lumber.

Cedar, although more expensive, will last for years. Fir will tend to rot after time. After mixing the substrate, pile it into a heap and let it sit undisturbed. After a week, turn the heap over and continue to turn it every 2 days until the manure has lost its odor and the mix is crumbly. This is when the substrate is ready to use. Alternately, you can buy ready-mixed mushroom compost from a garden center or nursery of a commercial mushroom grower and use that instead of prepared manure.

2' deep cedar bin for preparing the manure substrate

b) **WHAT KIND TO GROW**: The seeds of mushrooms, called spawn, are available for purchase from suppliers, or you can buy kits that come complete with the growing medium. The type of spawn determines the type of mushroom you will grow. Kits make growing mushrooms easy because they come with growing material that's been inoculated with mushroom spores. Kits will produce mushrooms often for six months, and several varieties are available. So which variety to buy?

1) **OYSTER MUSHROOMS**: This variety can be grown easily, and can be purchased in mushroom kits from suppliers. Oyster mushrooms are a delicately flavored and textured mushroom that are best grown during the warmer months. They come in three shades: pink, blue, and the traditional white and brown.

2) GOURMET MUSHROOMS: Gourmet mushrooms can easily be grown in the BIODOME GARDEN by purchasing kits from online suppliers. These kits include pre-sterilized bags of mushroom growing medium and syringes prefilled with mushroom spores of shiitake, enoki, oyster, chestnut, Swiss brown, shaggy mane, and others, and all you have to do is to keep the bed moist, clean and dark.

3) BUTTON MUSHROOMS: These mushrooms are the most common mushroom found in super markets. They are easy to grow, heartier than others, and less susceptible to fluctuations in temperature.

c) BUILD THE MUSHROOM FLAT: In an open, airy environment like the BIODOME GARDEN it's good to enclose the mushroom flat to prevent draughts and fluctuations of temperature and atmospheric moisture. A lid on the mushroom flat works well for this purpose, and for boxing the mushrooms in total darkness. 1"x8" cedar makes a frame to fit the area beneath the utility sink in the BIODOME GARDEN. This should be about 24"x30". You can use 1"x12" cedar boards, cut to 30" lengths, for the bottom of the flat. A lid made from exterior plywood can be cut to size and placed over the bin to hold in the moisture and keep it dark while the mushrooms grow. In order to maintain a uniform temperature, the lid can also be lined with a thin sheet of rigid foam insulation and cut to a size that fits down inside the flat so the lid can close.

d) PLANT THE SPAWN: When the manure mix is crumbly, fill the mushroom flat with the substrate and sprinkle the spawn on top. Don't turn it under. For mushrooms to grow, the temperature in the area where the flat is should be about 70 degrees Fahrenheit. In about three weeks the spawn will have rooted, and filaments will have spread into the substrate. This interwoven mat is called the mycelium, and it's the main part of the fungus. What we eat is the fruiting bodies of the fungus. When the mycelium appear, raise the lid and expose them to light, lower the temperature by spraying the mycelium and substrate, and close the lid. Do this daily during the next week.

e) MUSHROOM GROWTH: Each day, check the bed by lifting the lid and spraying the surface. In a week, small mushrooms will pop their heads. When the mushroom caps are fully opened and separated from the stems, they will be ready to eat. If conditions remain constant and conducive to growth, they will continue to produce for three months.

f) MONITOR THE TEMPERATURE: Sudden changes in temperature must be avoided, which is why an insulated lid over the mushroom flat is good. A dry floor under the flat is imperative because a wet floor chills the substrate and makes it unhealthy for the spawn. If necessary, place a couple of 1"x12" cedar boards under the flat. The temperature of the interior of a mushroom bed should be about 60° F during the growing period, and the temperature of the surface of the bed between 45° to 50° F. If the temperature goes lower, mycelium will have a tendency to rest, and the crop will stagnate. When cold weather sets in, cover the flat to keep the substrate warm.

(3) UTILIZING THE MUSHROOM COMPOST: Mushroom compost that has already been used for growing mushrooms is good for soil improvement, especially in vegetable gardens, because it is high in organic content. Vegetables grow best where the soil tends toward alkaline, especially for the *brassicas* (kale, Brussels sprouts, cabbage, cauliflower and broccoli), as these are less likely to be infected by clubroot disease. But don't overuse the mushroom compost because it can lead to increased soil alkalinity, and plant growth will suffer, causing yellowing of leaves and foliage, growth stunt, and reduction in fruiting. Alternatively, mushroom compost can restore acid soils low in organic matter.

10 BLOCKS, STONES OR STAVES

Beauty is in the eye of the beholder

The BIODOME GARDEN on the cover of this book is constructed using concrete silo staves. When used for the walls for the raised vegetable beds, and especially when constructing the fish tank, silo staves offer strength unparalleled by landscape building blocks, and are especially economic. Staves are available around the country and can be located by making an "advanced search" on Google on "concrete silo staves." But for real economy, concrete staves from old and abandoned silos are often sold cheaply through local farm and ranch newspapers, or even offered for free on Craigslist or other classified listings, just for hauling them away. But the tradeoff for the strength of a silo-stave BIODOME GARDEN is the beauty and flexibility in design of curved landscaping stones. Building and garden centers around the country offer a plethora of blocks and stones for everything from retaining walls, to curved planter beds, to small circles around trees, and to whatever height you desire. For the purpose of this book, however, we will only consider building-block systems that do not need special foundation preparation, other than a bed of gravel.

(1) CONCRETE SILO STAVES: Concrete silo staves are small, precast concrete blocks with ridged grooves along each edge that lock them together into a high strength shell. When moving up vertically, as when adding a second course of silo staves for building the fish tank in the BIODOME GARDEN, one end of the stave is concave while the other is convex, allowing the blocks to interconnect.

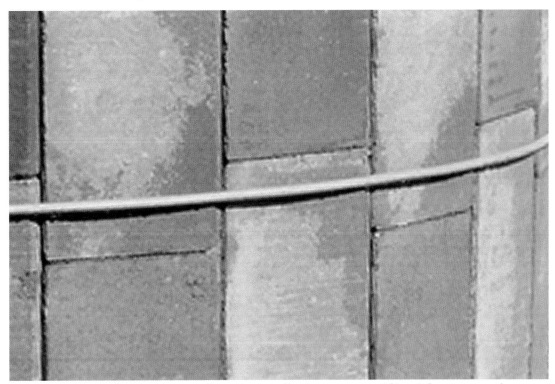

Section of a concrete silo stave wall... beauty sacrificed for strength

The staves used for the BIODOME GARDEN on the cover of the book are 10" wide and 30" tall, with a thickness of 2-1/2". Concrete silo staves are similar to concrete landscaping blocks in that they are individual building blocks that can be assembled without the aid of expensive equipment, and without a need for a team of workers. But whereas concrete provides the primary structural integrity for concrete blocks, it's the hoops with silo staves that provide the primary structural integrity of the wall being assembled.

Each course of silo staves is held together by means of an exterior steel hoop that encircles and compresses the staves into a tight ring. These hoops, or curved steel rods, are made up of sections that are joined by special lugs, which are also used for tightening.

Lugs are used to connect the sections of hoop and tighten the ring

The hoops are composed of two or more sections, the number of sections being determined by the diameter of the structure being assembled. The outer wall of the BIODOME GARDEN required three sections of hoop, whereas the staves for the fish tank required only two. After the course of staves is completed, the hoops are drawn tight. The stave walls of the vegetable bed need nothing more, but after the walls of the fish tank are assembled and the hoops are tightened, the interior of the tank will need a coating of cement mortar to seal the joints and prevent the tank from leaking, and also to produce a smooth surface.

(2) **LANDSCAPING STONES**: The arrangement of landscape stones in the photo below was one set up at a garden center, but it's a sample of what can be done in an afternoon, with a couple of people at work. The blocks need no mortar, but you should prepare the ground where the BIODOME GARDEN will sit in the same way that you would prepare it for using concrete silo staves, including setting down a 4" base of 3/4" crushed rock, which should be leveled and tamped before beginning. You will also need to trench and assemble all of the below-grade water and drain lines, as described and shown in the photos in Chapter 4.

Landscape stones, tapered for making a circle, with a granite texture

Following are samples of a few of the many types of landscaping stones that can be used for building the walls of your BIODOME GARDEN. A visit to a home and garden center will help you decide which way you want to go.

Landscaping stones come in unlimited colors and variations, some with sharp edges and angles, some smooth and "weather worn," and others more natural in appearance. Your choice. Here are a few more examples...

Your BIODOME GARDEN can be as "formal" or as "natural" as you want to make it. The blocks in the photo above were set in place using mortar and some concrete know-how. But by using native stones, as shown in the photo below, you can create a more natural appearance.

(3) PAVERS ADD BEAUTY: To keep your feet from getting soggy, you'll want to make pathways leading to and around the BIODOME GARDEN. Gravel, bark chips, and crushed nut shells work fine and are cheap and easy to put down. Pathways can be lined with cedar bender boards that are held in place with short stakes, and can curve to make a nice approach while containing whatever you choose to use as a pathway. But for a more attractive appearance, pavers can be put down.

Pavers for walkways are a great way to set off your BIODOME GARDEN

The photos above are only a small sampling of what's available at home and garden centers all around the country. The following is a brief tutorial on putting down pavers for a walkway to the BIODOME GARDEN:

a) **SITE PREPARATION**: Determine the elevation you'll want for the pathway by using stakes and string. If you want your pavers to sit on top of the ground, that's fine, but you might prefer that they be set down some to prevent people from tripping. In that case, the soil will need to be excavated to the depth desired and the ground checked against a string line that you can stretch between stakes at the finish height of the pavers. Setting a sample paver in place as you go will insure a correct finish height.

b) **PREPARE THE BASE**: If the soil beneath where you have scraped or excavated is loose, tamp it down to compact it.

c) **INSTALL EDGE RESTRAINT**: This is to outline the pathway and hold the pavers in place. This can be done using concrete curbing, or cedar edging or bender board, which is held in place with short stakes.

d) **PUT DOWN A BASE**: On top of the tamped soil, put down a 2-3" layer of 1/2" crushed rock and tamp it down. On top of this will be a bed of sand to a maximum depth of 1". The sand can be leveled by dragging a 2x4 board along the top of the edge restraints.

d) **LAY DOWN THE PAVERS**: Lay down the first paver in a corner of the walkway, then work your way out, in a triangular direction, laying each new paver against the previously-placed paver, while sliding it down.

e) **SWEEP SAND INTO THE CRACKS**: Use paver sand to fill in the spaces between the pavers. Alternately, you can sweep dry concrete mortar into the cracks and hose it down to form a more solid walkway.

Pavers can be laid square, in herringbone patterns, or in random patterns. They can be laid to give a formal look or an old-world cobbled look, and be laid from rustic to traditional and contemporary. A little landscaping to set off your new BIODOME GARDEN, and you will have a place that will bring you joy, along with fresh herbs, vegetables or flowers, for years to come.

A bed of gravel is laid out in preparation for putting down landscape pavers

(20) HAVE FUN!: Your BIODOME GARDEN can be as much a part of your living environment as you want to make it. You can have a completely functional unit, bare of all but the necessities, such as a gravel walkway approach and gravel around the perimeter to keep down the weeds, or you can accent your BIODOME GARDEN with landscape pavers and shrubs and let your imagination take you to wherever your pocketbook will allow. Landscape design books offer ideas you might not be able to dream up yourself. But whatever you decide, your BIODOME GARDEN will be uniquely yours, and before long, it will be overflowing with an abundance of nutritious, pesticide-free produce.

The End

HELPFUL WEBSITES

FIBERGLASS DOMES

http://www.fsiweb.com/products.asp?UnitNo=dome16S&Index=domes
http://www.geodesic-greenhouse-kits.com/small_greenhouses.php
http://www.domesheltersystem.com/
http://www.kacperpostawski.com/products.html

SILO STAVES

http://www.macraesbluebook.com/search/product_company_list.cfm?Prod_Code=9009445
http://moy-mir.biz/base/cat.php?q=concrete-silo-staves
http://www.macraesbluebook.com/search/product_company_list.cfm?prod_code=9009445&region=Minnesota-MN
http://www.macraesbluebook.com/search/company.cfm?company=444935
http://www.slsilo.com/
http://www.mcphersonconcrete.com/co-storage-systems.htm
http://www.mariettasilos.com/?gclid=CNKO2uP_v6kCFQI3gwodbl_qgw

LANDSCAPING STONES

http://www.landscapingnetwork.com/ponds/
http://www.keystonewalls.com
http://www.mutualmaterials.com

FISH TANK AND/OR COMPONENTS

http://www.mcphersonconcrete.com/pipe-specs.htm (section of concrete culvert)
http://www.tank-depot.com/productdetails.aspx?part=TC7246AA
http://www.watertanks.com/products/0110-160.asp (1350 gal; $625; no photo)

GROWING MUSHROOMS

http://www.ehow.com/how_6364924_raise-mushrooms-home.html
http://everythingmushrooms.com/shop/
http://www.ehow.com/how_6364924_raise-mushrooms-home.html#ixzz1PC7o1dOu
http://www.shroomsnmore.com
http://www.sporepros.com
http://www.fengfu.com.cn
http://www.GardensAlive.com
http://www.mrcashop.org/mushroom

AQUACULTURE (FISH AND PLANTS)
http://www.mybackachers.com/aquaponics.htm
http://www.landscapingnetwork.com/ponds/
http://www.pondplants1.com/planting_instructions.htm
http://www.azgardens.com/c-15-freshwater-aquarium-plants.aspx
http://www.hardypondplants.com/
http://www.koiphen.com/forums/register.php?

MUSHROOM COMPOST
http://apps.rhs.org.uk/advicesearch/profile.aspx?pid=294
http://www.gardenguides.com/115358-raise-mushrooms-home.html
http://www.mybackachers.com/mushrooms_raising.htm
https://attra.ncat.org/attra-pub/summaries/mushroom.html
http://www.greencenteracres.com/id34.html
http://www.ehow.co.uk/how_7572724_make-mushroom-spawn-home.html
http://www.ehow.co.uk/how_7725725_grow-edible-mushrooms-inside.html
http://www.booksfiction.biz/index.php?b=Mushrooms_how_to_grow_them&page=3

EARTHWORMS
http://www.tpwmagazine.com/archive/2002/mar/skillbuilder/
http://www.redwormcomposting.com/general-questions/lots-of-mold-in-my-worm-bin/
http://www.redwormcomposting.com/raising-earth-worms/
http://www.piteraq.dk/ecology/earthworm.html

ORGANIC PEST CONTROL
http://www.extremelygreen.com/pestcontrolguide.cfm
http://www.ghorganics.com/page9.html
http://www.ghorganics.com/page14.html
http://www.ghorganics.com/Page44.html

AUTHOR'S NOTE ABOUT THE FIBERGLASS DOME: Because I have had so many inquiries about the availability of the dome, and the problem of finding one that is adaptable for a BIODOME GARDEN, as well as being affordable, I am currently in the process of manufacturing a 16' diameter dome, similar to the one on the cover, which will be made specifically for a BIODOME GARDEN. The dome will be made up of eight panels that will interlock along the edges and connect together with bolts, two panels of which will have large vents (as shown), and one will have a "walk through" door--a new feature. The fiberglass will contain a UV inhibitor for longevity and a slight bluish cast for attractiveness. For information on the availability of the dome, please go to **www.biodomegreenhouse.com**. There is a "contact" box where you can add your name, if you would like to be notified when the domes are available for purchase.

Made in the USA
Lexington, KY
18 August 2012